T0086591

A RHYTHMIC *TWIST*
TRIPLET CONCEPTS
FOR DRUMSET
By Jeff Salem

Edited by Joe Bergamini

Book Design and Music Engraving by Rick Gratton

Executive Producers: Paul Siegel and Rob Wallis

Cover Design by Mike Hoff

Front and Back Cover Photo by Neal Burstyn

Photos by Philippe Lapointe, Rob McNeil, Jamie Quaile and Mark Kovich

Audio tracks recorded by Jeff Salem, Richi Vetro & Casey Manierka-Quaile

Jeff Salem's Music Studio
http://www.jsmusicstudio.com
http://www.salemdrum.com
http://drumsinu.com

Catalog HDBK27/HL6620154
ISBN: 9781423496342

HUDSON MUSIC®

ACKNOWLEDGMENTS

Many thanks and love to my wife Helen for all her continuous support, and to my parents for never taking my drumsticks away from me.

Special thanks to:

Rob Wallis, Paul Siegel, Joe Bergamini, and the rest of Hudson Music team for believing in my concepts and allowing me to write this book.

Richi Vetro and Casey Manierka-Quaile for their contributions to the play-alongs on the accompanying CD.

Big thanks to all my students for listening to my ideas and concepts for the last 19 years.

Thanks to my good friend Matt McFarland for his loyalty, commitment, and dedication to the art form of drumming. To all the teachers at J.S. Music Studio who provide a superior quality of expertise and passion for teaching.

To all the great teachers I have had over to the course of my career, sharing their wisdom, knowledge, and support: Dan Bodanis, Dom Famularo, Rick Gratton, Robin Boers, Vito Rezza, Jim Chapin and many other great drummers who have shared their ideas on stage at clinics as well as in their books and DVDs.

To David Harvey from Drummer's Choice for his continuous support and for giving me my first opportunity to teach.

To all the wonderful people at Sabian, Vic Firth, Yamaha, Evans , Roland, and LP for their support.

Last but not least, thanks to my two favorite 4-legged friends, Buddy and Barney, for the early-morning and late-night strolls.

ABOUT THE CD

All the examples in this book are in MP3 format and were recorded live with no Pro Tools editing involved. What you hear is what was played—no moving notes around or adjusting tempos. I used my Roland TD-12 module with Cakewalk Sonar software. For each of the chapters I used a different drum set setting from the TD-12.

All the tracks were recorded to a click at various tempos with a one-bar count off on the hi-hat. The track number on the CD is written beside each example in the book. Some tracks contain multiple examples.

For the drum fills, I recorded one of the following arrangements:
1 One bar fill/one bar time
2 Two bars fill/two bars time
3 One bar fill/three bars time
4 Four bars fill

I supported most of the fills with the various foot ostinatos shown on pages 27 and 60.

To support the fills, I used many grooves from the various styles I demonstrated in the Triplet-Based Grooves section as well as ideas from the Grooves and Applications chapter.

For all of the grooves I recorded four bars of each example.

PLAY-ALONG TRACKS
There are 13 play-along tracks based on the many different triplet grooves and styles that are introduced in the beginning of the book. They are all approximately 2 minutes long. These are just exercises for you to try the many different ideas in the book to help develop your swing playing. Jam out and have fun!

Listed below are the play-along examples and track numbers from the CD.

Track 165: Slow Blues 12/8 - 74 BPM. (**B**eats **P**er **M**inute)
Track 166: Blues Shuffle - 100 BPM.
Track 167: Beach Shuffle - 125 BPM.
Track 168: Funk Shuffle - 140 BPM.
Track 169: Medium Swing - 140 BPM.
Track 170: Medium/Up Swing -160 BPM.
Track 171: Jump Swing - 180 BPM.
Track 172: Up Swing - 200 BPM.
Track 173: Hip-Hop - 190 BPM.
Track 174: Afro-Cuban - 110 BPM.
Track 175: Afro-Cuban - 190 BPM. in 6/8 time
Track 176: Reggae - 130 BPM.
Track 177: Reggae - 160 BPM.

Tracks 165,166, 167,168,169,170,171,172,175, and**177** written and performed by Richi Vetro

Tracks 173,174, and **176** written and performed by Casey Manierka-Quaile

INSIDE THIS BOOK

BIOGRAPHY _____ 4

DRUM KEY _____ 4

WHAT ARE TRIPLETS? _____ 5

    Triplet Warm-Up Exercise 6

TRIPLET-BASED GROOVES AND STYLES _____ 7

    12/8 Grooves 7

    Shuffles 8

    Basic 2-4 Shuffle Groove 8

    Half-Time Shuffle 9

    Jazz 10

    Hip-Hop 12

    World 14

    Eighth-Note Triplets And Variarions 16

A RHYTHMIC TWIST CONCEPT _____ 18

    A Creative Approach To Triplet-Based Fills and Grooves 18

CHAPTER 1 - Fills with Alternate Sticking and No Rests _____ 22

CHAPTER 2 - Fills and Grooves Adding One Bass Drum Note _____ 28

    Drum Fills 28

    Groove Builders 28

CHAPTER 3 - Fills and Grooves Adding Two Bass Drum Notes _____ 34

    Drum Fills 34

    Grooves 34

CHAPTER 4 - Paraddidle Ideas _____ 40

    Drum Fills 41

    Grooves and Jazz Ideas 43

CHAPTER 5 - Combination Fill and Groove Ideas _____ 48

CHAPTER 6 - Fills with Rests _____ 53

    Sixteenth-Note Rhythms Converted To Eighth-Note Triplets 53

    Fills with Rests 55

    Foot Ostinatos 60

CHAPTER 7 - Thirty-Second Notes To Sixteenth-Note Triplet Ideas _____ 61

    Warm-Up Exercises 61

CHAPTER 8 - Combination Ideas, Fills and Grooves _____ 66

GROOVES AND APPLICATIONS _____ 71

RECOMMENDED BOOKS AND DVDs _____ 75

BIOGRAPHY

Jeff Salem is an internationally recognized drummer based in Toronto, Canada, who has performed in over 70 countries. His professional career started in his late teens, performing and recording with well-known rock bands including Fist (A&M), Sword (Aquarius), Saints & Sinners (Savage/BMG), Lee Aaron (Attic), Randy Bachman, Robben Ford, Coop-De-Ville, Kalan Porter ("Canadian Idol" Winner 2004), and many other artists. Jeff has also performed on many cruise ships, both in the orchestra as well as a bandleader. Known to be a versatile drummer, performing and reading all styles of music, Jeff had the opportunity to perform on a millennium cruise to Antarctica working with various artists including The Chieftains, Diana Krall, Natalie McMaster, Art Garfunkel and actor Dan Ackroyd.

Highly active in music education, Jeff performs percussion workshops and clinics for students of all grades. Through his program "Music is My Passion," Jeff has become a public motivational speaker, inspiring students to learn a musical instrument. He has delivered this performance to over 500 schools in the past 15 years. Jeff is also involved with the program P.L.A.S.P. (Peel Lunch & After School Program). He offers his hand drumming clinic performance "A Little Drumming In Everyone" to this program. It caters to youths between the ages of 4 and 12. Jeff is also the creator and founder of the group ENVIRO DRUM. This band creates percussion music with recyclable products similar to the group STOMP. Enviro Drum has been performing concerts at many schools.

An active author, Jeff has released 3 instructional videos: *Groove-A Diddles, Drumology* and *Double Bass Vocabulary – Vol.1*, and an instructional funk book, *Messin Wid Da Bull* (Hudson Music). He has performed at many music trade shows including the NAMM show both in Anaheim, CA and Nashville, TN; Musicmesse in Frankfurt, Germany; Music West in Vancouver, BC; Cape Breton International Drumfest in Sydney, Nova Scotia; OMEA; Arts Alive; Guitar Workshop Plus; The Collective in NYC; and Canadian Music Week in Toronto, ON. Jeff is a freelance writer for the magazines *Canadian Musician* and *Modern Drummer*, and also maintains a large roster of students for private instruction at his studio, J.S. Music Studio in Brampton, ON.

Jeff Salem endorses Yamaha Drums, Sabian Cymbals, Vic Firth Drumsticks, Evans Drumheads, Latin Percussion, and HQ Percussion (Real Feel Pads).

Visit his websites at:

www.salemdrum.com   www.jsmusicstudio.com   www.drumsinu.com

DRUM KEY

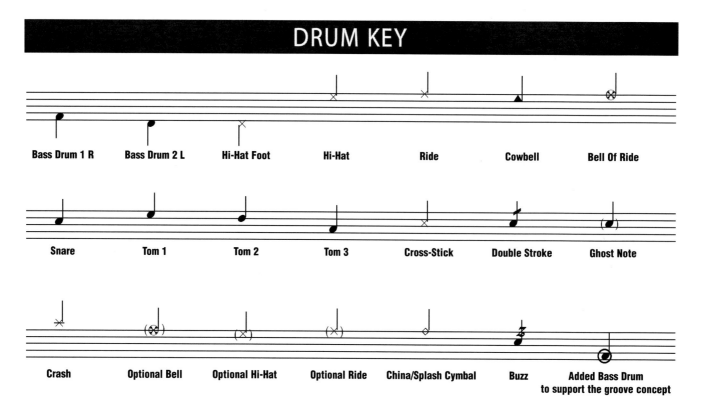

To keep things simple and effective, the 8th-note triplet will be used as the main rhythmic pattern throughout these exercises. There are other kinds of triplets, but we won't be using them in this book.

Eighth-note triplets are defined as *three notes played evenly in the space of one quarter note*. They are grouped together as three 8th notes with a number 3 written over top of each grouping. In one bar of 4/4 time we would have 4 groupings of 8th-note triplets, which equals a total of (12) 8th notes in the bar (see example A). I have written **1 T L 2 T L 3 T L 4 T L** to represent 1 triplet, 2 triplet, 3 triplet, 4 triplet.

Example A

Quite often you will see the same number of notes written in 12/8 time as shown in (example B).

Example B

Both look a little different and are counted different, but sound the same. If the tempo is fast, counting in 12/8 can be quite challenging, so it's easier to hear and feel the flow of the three notes written as triplets in 4/4 time.

The first challenge I and many of my students experienced when I started playing drums was to get comfortable with the feel and flow of the three notes to a quarter-note. Let's face it, 3 is an odd number, and when playing hand to hand on the snare you will notice the downbeat will land on a different hand each quarter-note.

Example C1

When playing 8th notes or 16th notes, if you start with the right hand, each downbeat will be played with the right hand. (Example C2, C3) (Downbeats are written with accents.)

Example C2

Example C3

TRIPLET WARM-UP EXERCISE

Try playing exercises 1 and 2 with the metronome at 60BPM. Once you are comfortable, try 80, 100, 120, 140, 160, or 180 BPM. The purpose of this exercise is to get you comfortable playing quarters, 8th notes, triplets and 16th notes and to be able to shift gears rhythmically while keeping your time steady. Alternate your hands on these exercises and count out loud. The goal is to be able to feel a strong quarter-note pulse as you play through the various note values.

Exercise 1

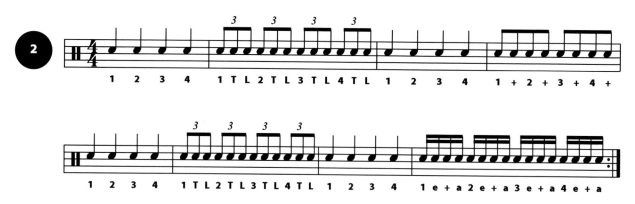

Exercise 2

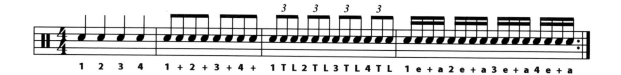

A TINY TALK

It is important to invest in a good metronome or drum machine. Many makes and models allow you to set not just only a quarter-note pulse, but different note values, allowing you to create different rhythms.

I use a Boss DB90 which has little sliders of eighths, sixteenths, and triplets. If you are using a metronome that has this type of feature, set it to triplets, or if using a drum machine, program triplets. This will help you hear and lock into playing the 3 notes per quarter-note.

Once you are comfortable with the concept and timing of the triplets, proceed to the next section, Triplet-Based Grooves and Styles.

12/8 Grooves

It was probably my 2nd or 3rd lesson when my drum teacher invited a guitar player to sit in our class, and he said, "We are going to jam."

The guitar player started playing a slow, bluesy idea similar to Joe Walsh's "Rocky Mountain Way." I remember playing a triplet-based groove.

Example 1

I will never forget how cool it felt to be able to play something that fit with the guitar part. My teacher looked at me and said, "Come on Jeff, throw in a drum fill!" Of course when I went for it I totally trained-wrecked the song. I defaulted to playing an 8th- and 16th-note fill, which broke the groove and ruined my timing. I asked myself, "Why did this happen?" The bottom line was that I never spent much time listening to music in this feel. Besides practicing this type of groove, it's equally important to listen to music in this feel.

Here are some recommended songs to listen to with this feel:

1. **"At Last"** - Etta James

2. **"What a Wonderful World"** - Louie Armstrong

3. **"Red House"** - Jimi Hendrix

4. **"Can't Help Falling in Love"** - Elvis Presley

5. **"Unchained Melody"** - The Righteous Brothers

6. **"Fallin'"** - Alicia Keys

7. **"King of the Blues"** - B.B. King

8. **"Texas Flood"** - Stevie Ray Vaughan

9. **"Hold the Line"** - Toto

10. **"Breakaway"** - Kelly Clarkson

Start by playing at a slow tempo (45BPM) and count out loud. Once you feel relaxed with the groove—or as I like to say, you own the groove—increase the tempo by 10 BPM, working up to 80 BPM. Try this basic beat and some of the other 12/8 variations in the Grooves and Applications chapter with the 12/8 play-along on the CD.

SHUFFLES

Many classic rock, new rock, pop, blues, funk and country songs are written with a shuffle feel. The shuffle rhythm is a groove where we play the first and third note of the 8th-note triplet.

Start off with your metronome at 40 BPM, using the triplet setting. (If you have a metronome that only plays quarter notes, set it to 120 BPM and count each pulse as 1-trip-let, 2-trip-let, 3-trip-let, 4-trip-let.) Make sure you only play the 1st and 3rd note. Try playing example 1 with (a) alternate sticking, (b) right hand only, (c) left hand only, and (d) both hands together.

The challenge for most students when first trying to play this rhythm is the tendency to shift back into a straight feel. Of paramount importance is to make the rhythm swing. To help students achieve this feel, I get them to say this phrase: Play-up/down-up/down-up/down-up/down-up, etc. (Only use the word "play" to start the shuffle cycle.)

Example 1

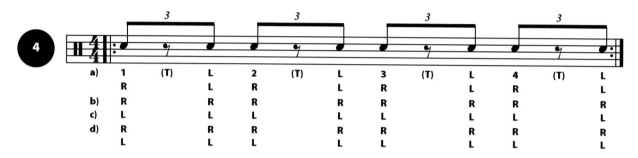

Example 2

Let's take a look at a basic shuffle beat. There are many shuffle styles, such as the Texas, the Chicago, the New Orleans, rock, and country shuffles. For the purposes of this book, we are going to focus mostly on the basic 2-4 and half-time shuffles. These are the foundation for all shuffle grooves.

BASIC 2-4 SHUFFLE GROOVE

Example 3

Example 3 is your basic 2-4 shuffle beat with the bass drum on beats 1 & 3 and the snare on 2 & 4. The shuffle rhythm is written on the ride cymbal but can be played on the hi-hat.

Count out loud, or say the words "up/down." Start at about 80 BPM. When comfortable, increase the tempo. Practice this groove with the shuffle play-alongs on the included disc. Try to lock in with the bass guitar on this track, and make your ride or hi-hat hand swing. When you feel comfortable, try some of the other shuffle grooves in the Grooves and Applications chapter.

The first shuffle song that I ever played was "You Shook Me" by Led Zeppelin. This song has a nice, slow, bluesy feel to it and is a great song for beginners to practice with. Here is a list of some classic shuffle tunes:

1. **"Tore Down"** - Eric Clapton

2. **"Some Kind of Wonderful"** - Grand Funk Railroad

3. **"Tush"** - ZZ Top

4. **"Reelin' in the Years"** - Steely Dan

5. **"Higher Ground"** - Stevie Wonder/Red Hot Chili Peppers

6. **"The Way You Make Me Feel"** - Michael Jackson

7. **"Lido Shuffle"** - Boz Scaggs

8. **"Cold Shot"** - Stevie Ray Vaughan

9. **"Boot Scootin' Boogie"** - Brooks & Dunn

10. **"Don't Stop Thinkin' About Tomorrow"** - Fleetwood Mac

HALF-TIME SHUFFLE

This is one of my all-time favorite grooves. The basic half-time shuffle beat has the snare on beat 3 and the bass drum on beat 1.

Example 4

Start by playing this groove slowly, at 80 BPM, ensuring that the h-ihat or ride cymbal has a nice, steady, swinging flow, and make sure to accent the snare on beat 3. When comfortable, increase the tempo gradually. Most songs in this feel are in the tempo range of 120-180 BPM.

Example 5 is a great exercise to get your hands used to feeling the shuffle flow. This exercise will also help develop your ghost notes.

Example 5

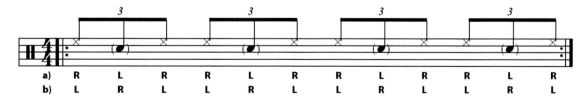

There are many other variations of this groove with syncopated bass and snare drum patterns that will sound funky. Some of these variations are featured in the Grooves and Applications chapter. Try the basic groove and its variations with the half-time shuffle play-along.

The first time I heard Jeff Pocaro drumming on the track "Rosanna," by Toto, I was captivated with his feel and the way the groove flowed.

Here is a list of a few classic half time shuffle tunes to check out:

1. **"Babylon Sisters"** - Steely Dan

2. **"Home at Last"** - Steely Dan

3. **"Fool in the Rain"** - Led Zeppelin

4. **"When the World Ends"** - The Dave Matthews Band

5. **"Bad Day"** - Daniel Powter

6. **"Rosanna"** - Toto

JAZZ

Jazz is primarily based around triplet phrasing. The ride cymbal and hi-hat foot are the two key instruments used. The ride cymbal pattern is based on a quarter-note pulse with triplet-phrased inflections.

Example 1 is the most common jazz ride pattern and can be called a basic swing feel. It is important to make this groove swing, as mentioned in the title of the classic jazz song "It Don't Mean A Thing (If It Ain't Got That Swing)."

Example 1

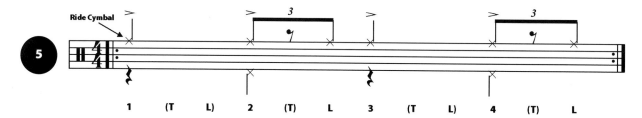

How Do We Get Students To Swing?

Well, the first thing many great teachers have told me is that we need to HEAR swing before we play it. Start listening to classic jazz tunes. Absorb the feel, dynamics, sounds and arrangement of the composition. Transferring your ideas to the instrument and making things swing might take some work, but here is the approach I use (I must thank drummer Ed Shaughnessy for this).

Many years ago, I attended a jazz workshop that Ed was teaching. His approach to getting students to swing their jazz ride cymbal pattern was to have them say the following phrase out loud: "Please-shut-the door-shut-the door-shut-the door-shut-the," etc. Only use the word "please" when starting the groove (see Example 2).

Example 2

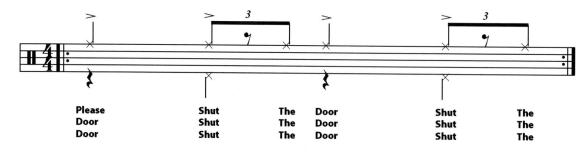

Since attending that workshop, I have used Ed's approach: Say it before you play it. I have had 10-year-old novice drummers able to play this feel by saying the words that Ed shared with me. Thank you Mr. Shaughnessy! A favorite part for me is when we say the word "shut" as the hi-hat shuts on beats 2&4.

Start off at 60 BPM and increase the tempo by 20 BPM increments up to 240BPM. Stay relaxed and make sure to feel the quarter-note pulse. Try this pattern with the jazz play-alongs on the CD.

Another great exercise is to have your snare hand play continous triplets throughout the bar with one hand while your ride cymbal and hi-hat play the traditional pattern. This will give you an accurate result of where the notes should fall on the ride cymbal. Make sure not to flam the notes.

Start off at 40 BPM for this exercise, and work your way up to about 120 BPM.

Example 3

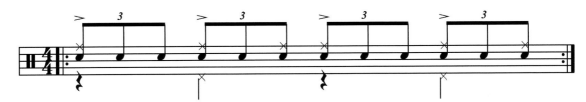

Working on these ideas, as well as listening to jazz on a regular basis, will help you develop a nice feel when playing this style. Patterns A-E outline other variations of the ride cymbal.

Try playing these examples by counting them as triplets as well as saying the phrase written below each exercise. You can practice all these ideas with the jazz play-alongs. There are also many other variations in the Grooves and Applications chapter.

Example 4a

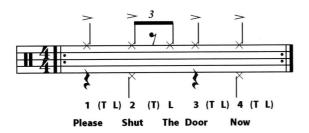

Example 4b

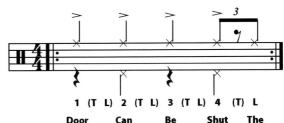

Example 4c

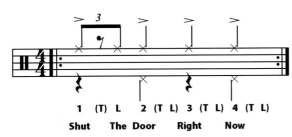

Example 4d

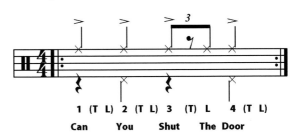

Example 4e

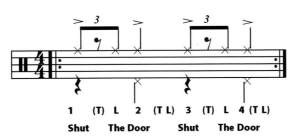

Further, try listening and playing along with these classic swing tunes.

Note: There are many artists that have recorded these classics. Please spend the time and explore the many recordings that are available.

1. **"Billie's Bounce"** - Charlie Parker

2. **"So What"** - Miles Davis

3. **"Take The "A" Train"** - Duke Ellington

4. **"In The Mood"** - Glenn Miller

5. **"Fly Me To The Moon"** - Frank Sinatra

6. **"It Don't Mean a Thing (If It Ain't Got That Swing)"** - Duke Ellington

7. **"Autum Leaves"** - Cannonball Adderley

8. **"Satin Doll"** - Duke Ellington

9. **"Freddie Freeloader"** - Miles Davis

10. **"Scrapple from the Apple"** - Charlie Parker

These are just a few of the thousands of great jazz pieces available. This language is a lifelong journey. Enjoy the ride and discovery of great jazz music.

HIP-HOP

Hip-hop music has become very popular in the last few decades. There are many different sub-categories and fusion genres of this style, such as new jack swing, hip house, rap, R&B, jungle, trip-hop, pop, and much more. Many songs in this style are based on a triplet swung feel, with the grooves written as combinations of a shuffle pattern using 16th-note triplets and 8th-note patterns. In this book, I have written a basic hip-hop groove as quarter notes and 8th-note triplets over two bars as shown in Example 1A, as opposed to the same groove written as 8th notes and 16th-note triplets over one bar (Example 1B). My reasoning for this is I feel that to support the concepts in this book, everything should be based on transforming 16th notes to 8th-note triplets. I find that hip-hop drummers have a great feel for playing jazz and vice versa, since the hi-hat patterns in hip-hop are rhythmically similar to the ride cymbal patterns in jazz. The only difference is the accents and dynamics, as well as the notes used to support the groove.

Example 1A   Basic hip-hop groove as quarter notes and 8th-note-triplets.

Example 1B   Same groove as above, but written with 8th- and 16th-note triplets.

While jazz music is primarily improvised, hip-hop is very structured. You might have to only play one groove for the entire song, but play it with great conviction, attitude, and consistency.

Practice basic grooves A-F with the hip-hop play-along, as well as some of the variations in the Grooves and Applications chapter.

Remember to count out loud, either saying the phrase written, or using the traditional triplet counting method. Don't forget to make these grooves swing.

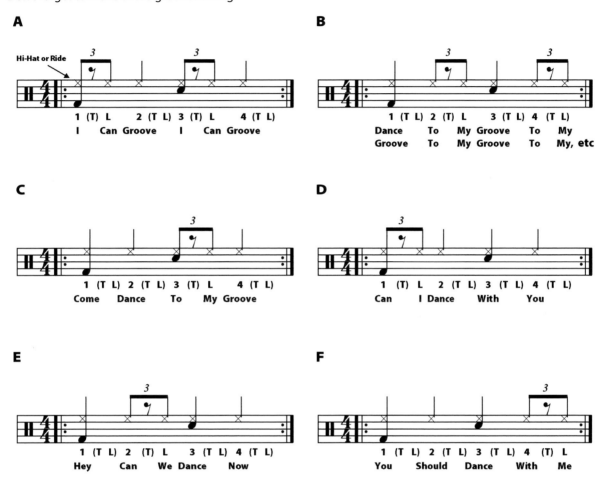

Crawford Lake, Ontario: Facilitating a drum circle, 2009

Here are a list of some songs from the last few decades that have a nice, bouncy, swung, hip-hop feel.

1. **"Superstition"** - Stevie Wonder

2. **"Sex Machine"** - James Brown

3. **"Lean on Me"** - Club Nouveau

4. **"Scar Tissue"** - The Red Hot Chili Pepper

5. **"True Colors"** - Phil Collins

6. **"Give In To Me"** - Michael Jackson

7. **"Turn Off the Light"** - Nelly Furtado

8. **"Love of My Life"** - Santana

9. **"Dream Lover"** - Mariah Carey

10. **"Waiting on the World to Change"** - John Mayer

As you can see, this list is quite diverse. The way I get students to develop this feel is to have them listen to many songs in this style. As they are doing so, I have them clap their hands and tap their feet throughout the tune, absorbing the swung feel.

WORLD

There are many other styles and grooves, such as the Afro-Cuban nanigo/bembe, that are based on a triplet feel and are usually written in 6/8 time.

Example 1 is a basic nanigo/bembe groove written as 8th-note triplets.

Example 1

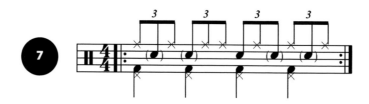

Check out these songs that feature a nanigo/bembe groove.

1. **"Alafia"** - Poncho Sanchez

2. **"Bembe Bakra"** - Bakra Bata

3. **"El Guapoen el Bembe"** - Gabriel Oscar Rosati

4. **"Bembe"** - Ricardo Estrada

5. **"Nanigo"** - Stevan Pasero

Many reggae songs are based on a swing feel, as well as a feel that falls in between triplets and straight 8th notes.

Example 2 is a basic reggae one-drop groove in 8th-note triplets.

Example 2

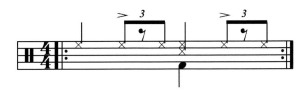

Check out these great reggae tunes:

1. **"One Love"** - Bob Marley

2. **"Ravers"** - Steel Pulse

3. **"Jamming"** - Bob Marley

4. **"Buffalo Soldier"** - Bob Marley

5. **"Equal Rights"** - Peter Tosh

More examples of these grooves will be shown later in this book, in the "Grooves & Applications" chapter.

Before playing to any of these World styles, spend time listening to the many great artists of these genres. Absorb their language of music, including the sounds, rhythms, feel, dynamics, and cultural background.

When you are comfortable, try playing to the nanigo/bembe and reggae play-alongs on the CD

At this point you should have an understanding of triplet-based grooves. Now let's go further by introducing fill ideas.

My cool, fun trash can band

EIGHTH-NOTE TRIPLETS AND VARIATIONS

1. Play all three notes.

2. Play the first two of the three notes.

③ 8

1 T L 2 T L 3 T L 4 T L

1 T (L) 2 T (L) 3 T (L) 4 T (L)

3. Play the last two of the three notes.

4. Play the first and third of the three notes.

Shuffle Rhythm

(1) T L (2) T L (3) T L (4) T L

1 (T) L 2 (T) L 3 (T) L 4 (T) L

5. Play the first of the three notes.

Sounds like quarter notes

1 (T L) 2 (T L) 3 (T L) 4 (T L)

6. Play the second of the three notes.

7. Play the last of the three notes.

(1) T (L) (2) T (L) (3) T (L) (4) T (L)

(1 T) L (2 T) L (3 T) L (4 T) L

Practice playing each pattern with alternate sticking on the snare drum, starting at 60 BPM. The goal is to get comfortable with all seven patterns before proceeding to the first chapter. Make sure to count out loud.

The next step is to apply these as simple drum fills around the drum kit. Apply each quarter-note value to a different drum. If you are using a 5-piece kit, beat 1 would fall on the snare, beat 2 on tom 1, beat 3 on tom 2, and beat 4 on tom 3.

Example 1   One-Bar Fill

R L R L R L R L R L R L

Try these 7 patterns with all of the previous grooves. Play three bars of time, then on the 4th bar play a one-bar drum fill. Don't forget to go through all 7 patterns as fill ideas, as shown in example 2.

Example 2 Shuffle beat with a drum fill.

Example 2 shows a basic shuffle beat, adding a crash cymbal on beat 1 of the first bar, with fill pattern number 3 on the 4th bar. Run through all 7 patterns with the 12/8 groove, basic shuffle, half-time shuffle, hip-hop, and World grooves daily, counting out loud. Start at a slow tempo and increase it gradually as you become more comfortable. At this point you are ready to enter the next stage where we twist things around.

Here we go!

Canada Day Performance 2009

A CREATIVE APPROACH TO TRIPLET-BASED FILLS AND GROOVES

The concept of this book is to offer drummers a creative and unique approach to playing triplet-based fills and grooves. In my teaching experiences I have found that most students have a much more difficult time in being creative with triplet-based ideas compared to 8th and 16th notes. Why is that?

I believe that growing up in North America, most beginner students are influenced by pop/rock music. A huge percentage of this style is based on a straight 8th and 16th notes. Most beginner students don't branch out to triplet-based feels and styles until they are comfortable in a straight feel (obviously there are some exceptions). I have had students influenced by jazz from moment one, but I would say 90%, if asked to improvise, will choose a straight feel. In a straight feel with pop and rock music, usually the quarter-note pulse is defined both in a groove or fill. It's easy to hear the downbeats. Plenty of triplet-based idea such as jazz will play off of the downbeat. The reason students feel more comfortable and confident with their own improvisational skills in a straight feel is because they are influenced by this feel. Simply, they can play more notes in a bar, so it is easier to improvise.

For example, in 4/4 time you can play sixteen 16th notes and have options of 15 broken variations from 1 to 4 notes per quarter-note value. In an 8th-note triplet feel in 4/4 time, you have 12 notes that can be played with the option of only 7 broken variations from 1-3 notes per quarter-note value.

With triplet-based fills, students tend to play it safe and seem to regurgitate the same fills over and over again, emphasizing the quarter-note pulse. *A Rhythmic Twist* will teach you an approach to being creative, versatile, confident, and original with fills and grooves off of the downbeat in 8th-note triplets.

Let's get started.

Example 1A demonstrates how we would count one bar of 16th notes. Example 1B demonstates a few ways that triplets can be counted. Please choose what's most comfortable for you. There is no right or wrong.

Example 1A

COUNTING SIXTEENTH NOTES

(9)

1 e + a 2 e + a 3 e + a 4 e + a

Example 1B

COUNTING EIGHTH-NOTE TRIPLETS

a) 1 T L 2 T L 3 T L 4 T L
b) 1 + a 2 + a 3 + a 4 + a
c) 1 e a 2 e a 3 e a 4 e a

COUNTING EXERCISE (Shifting gears from sixteenth notes to eighth-note triplets)

Example 2 displays one bar of 16th notes in 3/4 time with an accent written on the downbeat. Letter A shows how 16th notes are counted. Letter B shows how these same notes would be counted if we interpret them as triplets.

Try playing this exercise at the same tempo going back and forth counting one bar as 16th notes then the next as triplets without changing the accent placement. This can be quite challenging at first. Notice that in the triplet mode you will be accenting the half-note triplet. Throughout this book there will be many examples where quarter-note triplets and half-note triplets are the key pulses in the groove or fill.

Example 2

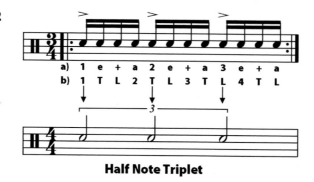

a) 1 e + a 2 e + a 3 e + a
b) 1 T L 2 T L 3 T L 4 T L

Half Note Triplet

Example 3 displays the breakdown of triplets.

Example 3

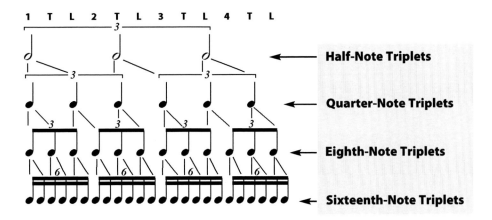

With every 16th-note example in 4/4 time, we can have 4 possible fills or grooves written as triplets. To understand this concept let's first look at a common 16th-note fill (1A), and a common 8th-note triplet fill (1B).

Example 1a Sixteenth-Note Fill

Example 1b Eighth-Note Triplet Fill

Note: If we write out the first 12 notes as 16th notes, the fill will be in 3/4 time.

RHYTHMIC POSITIONS

This is what I call the first position, using the first 12notes of the original fill in 4/4 time.

1a

Position   1   2   3 **from original fill**

This fill is written in the 2nd position, starting with beats 2, 3,4.

2b

Position   2   3   4 **from original fill**

This fill is written in the 3rd position, starting with beats 3, 4 then back to beat 1.

2c

Position   3   4   1 **from original fill**

This fill is written in the 4th position, starting with beat 4, and going back to beat 1 and 2.

2d

Position   4   1   2 **from original fill**

Now lets take these same examples and write the 12 notes out as 8th-note triplets using all four variations.

2a

2b

2c

2d

Master Class at The Collective, NYC, 2010

In this chapter we will focus on playing 8th-note triplet fills without any rests in the bar—12 notes alternating between your hands. If you are right-handed, start with the right hand, and if you are left-handed, begin with the left. I have deliberately left accents out, as I find with many of the variations from the original 16th-note fill you will feel different placements for the accents. These fills will get you comfortable at playing off of the downbeat. If we place an accent on every 4th note you will notice that the accent falls on the half-note triplet. The half-note triplet pulse emphasizes a 3-over-4 feel, which we will visit later in the book with some timing concepts. Start off slow with these fills, and try adding the following foot patterns 1-8 when comfortable.

SINGLE STROKE SIXTEENTH-NOTE FILLS TO EIGHTH-NOTE TRIPLETS WITH VARIATIONS

Note: Apply the single-stroke hand-to-hand (R L R L etc.) sticking to all the fills in this chapter.

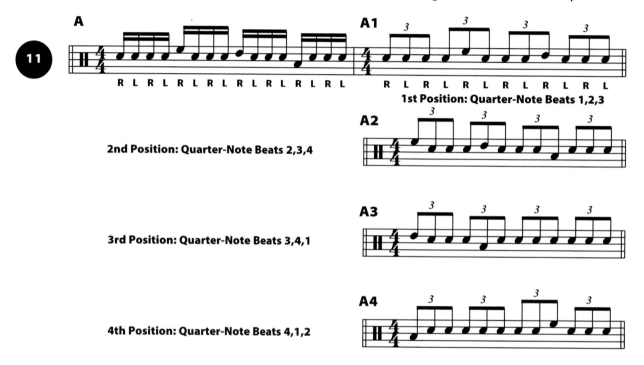

2nd Position: Quarter-Note Beats 2,3,4

3rd Position: Quarter-Note Beats 3,4,1

4th Position: Quarter-Note Beats 4,1,2

This grip isn't German, French or American.
It's the one and only Canadian grip!

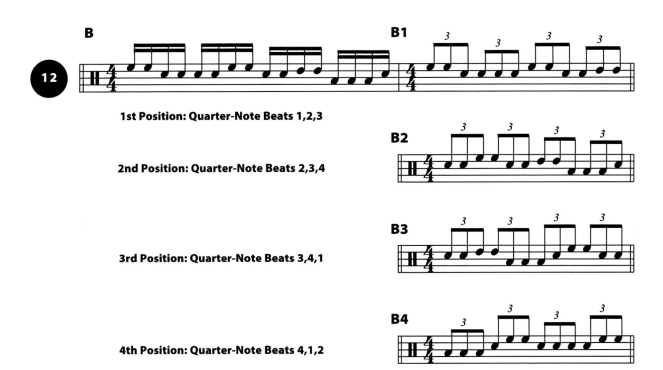

1st Position: Quarter-Note Beats 1,2,3

2nd Position: Quarter-Note Beats 2,3,4

3rd Position: Quarter-Note Beats 3,4,1

4th Position: Quarter-Note Beats 4,1,2

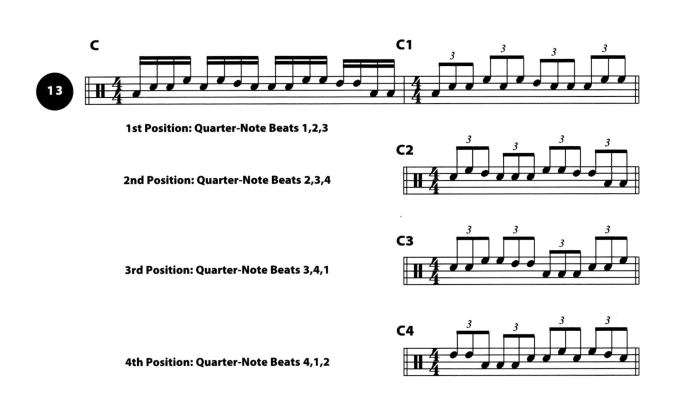

1st Position: Quarter-Note Beats 1,2,3

2nd Position: Quarter-Note Beats 2,3,4

3rd Position: Quarter-Note Beats 3,4,1

4th Position: Quarter-Note Beats 4,1,2

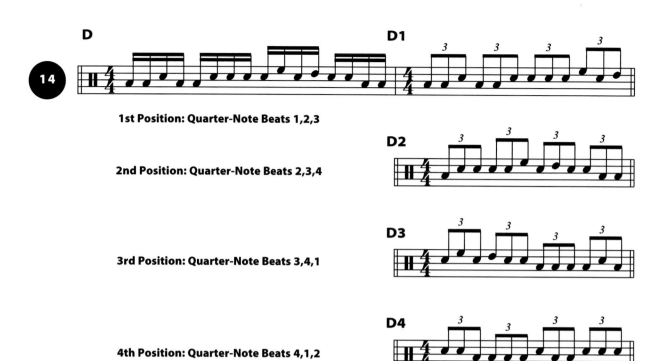

1st Position: Quarter-Note Beats 1,2,3

2nd Position: Quarter-Note Beats 2,3,4

3rd Position: Quarter-Note Beats 3,4,1

4th Position: Quarter-Note Beats 4,1,2

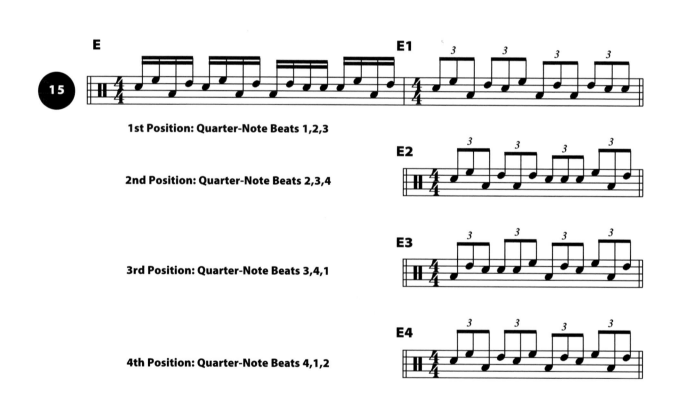

1st Position: Quarter-Note Beats 1,2,3

2nd Position: Quarter-Note Beats 2,3,4

3rd Position: Quarter-Note Beats 3,4,1

4th Position: Quarter-Note Beats 4,1,2

16

1st Position: Quarter-Note Beats 1,2,3

2nd Position: Quarter-Note Beats 2,3,4

3rd Position: Quarter-Note Beats 3,4,1

4th Position: Quarter-Note Beats 4,1,2

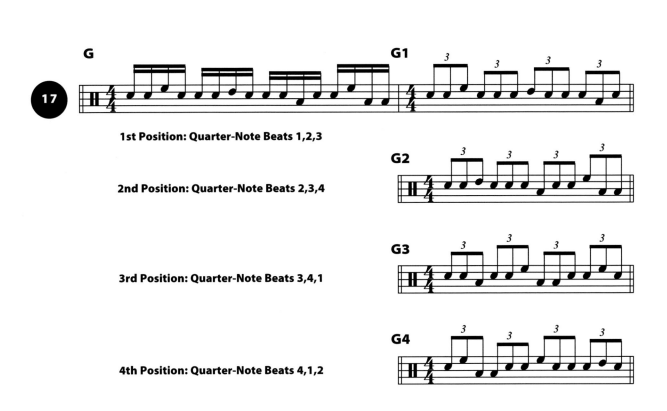

17

1st Position: Quarter-Note Beats 1,2,3

2nd Position: Quarter-Note Beats 2,3,4

3rd Position: Quarter-Note Beats 3,4,1

4th Position: Quarter-Note Beats 4,1,2

H **H1**

18

1st Position: Quarter-Note Beats 1,2,3

H2

2nd Position: Quarter-Note Beats 2,3,4

H3

3rd Position: Quarter-Note Beats 3,4,1

H4

4th Position: Quarter-Note Beats 4,1,2

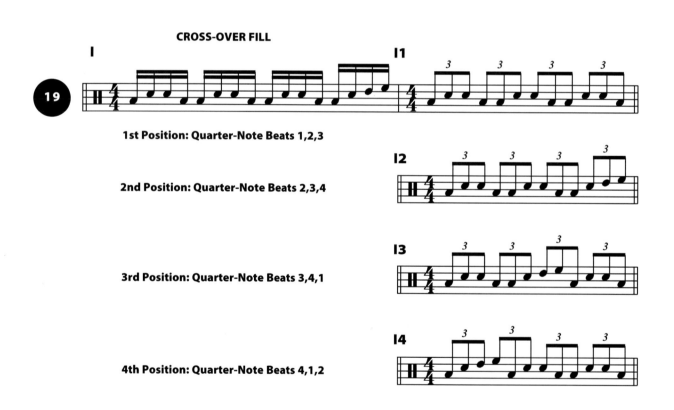

CROSS-OVER FILL

I **I1**

19

1st Position: Quarter-Note Beats 1,2,3

I2

2nd Position: Quarter-Note Beats 2,3,4

I3

3rd Position: Quarter-Note Beats 3,4,1

I4

4th Position: Quarter-Note Beats 4,1,2

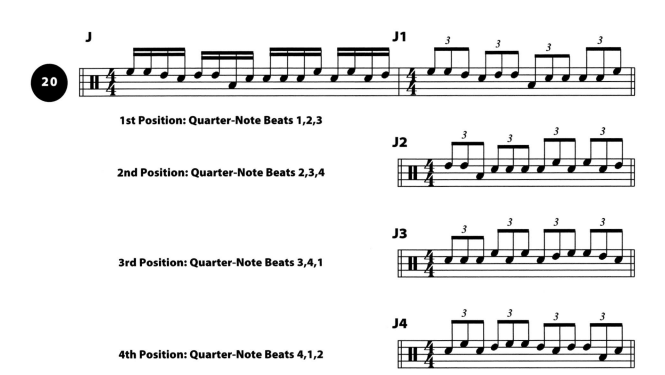

20

J **J1**

1st Position: Quarter-Note Beats 1,2,3

2nd Position: Quarter-Note Beats 2,3,4

J2

J3

3rd Position: Quarter-Note Beats 3,4,1

J4

4th Position: Quarter-Note Beats 4,1,2

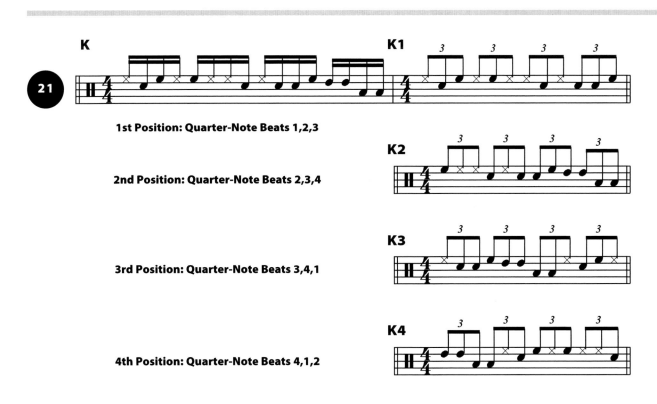

21

K **K1**

1st Position: Quarter-Note Beats 1,2,3

2nd Position: Quarter-Note Beats 2,3,4

K2

K3

3rd Position: Quarter-Note Beats 3,4,1

K4

4th Position: Quarter-Note Beats 4,1,2

FOOT PATTERNS

1   **2**   **3**   **4**

5   **6**   **7**   **8**

This chapter is divided into two parts; drums fills and grooves.

DRUM FILLS

The following drum fills have one bass drum played within four 16th notes (examples a-d).

It is important to follow the sticking pattern that is written. I wrote the patterns for a right-handed drummer; if you are left-handed just play the opposite sticking. All of the downbeats (numbers) and offbeats ("&'s") are played with the right hand, while the "e's" and "ah's" are played with the left. I have mixed these patterns with some alternate 16th notes as written in chapter one. Following this sticking pattern will help you develop a smooth and consistent method of playing these fills around the drumset.

GROOVE BUILDERS

In many of the chapters, we can take the original 16th-note pattern and create a groove. To convert the fill to a groove, the following steps must take place:

- Right hand plays on the hi-hat or the ride cymbal (if left handed, reverse the sticking).

- Sometimes we will bring the right hand onto the snare for the backbeat.

- Improvise with the bass drum in various places in the groove. Most of the bass drum notes added land with the hi-hat or ride cymbal.

- Experiment with accent placement. I have added accents where I feel they are suited. Please experiment with your own placement. I find that with each variation the backbeat and ghost note placement will feel different to everyone. Try different variations within the same groove

- When playing on the ride, add the hi-hat foot stroke on beats 2 and 4 for a jazz feel.

- Improvise with various open and closed hi-hat patterns.

Many of these grooves will have feels and influences of reggae, Afro-Cuban 6/8, jazz, shuffles, 12/8 and half-time shuffles.

These grooves will give you more options for playing a syncopated shuffle base groove, hearing the quarter-note-triplet pulse (6 over 4) with the right hand, as in example A4, in this chapter. Example C will emphasize the half-note-triplet pulse (3 over 4) on the bass drum.

Start off slow, and repeat each pattern several times before moving to the next.

ORIGINAL PATTERN

FILLS   GROOVES

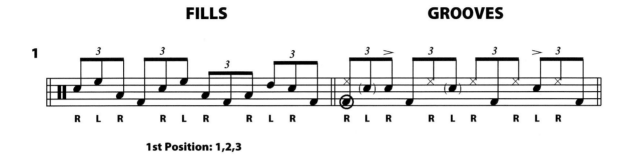

1st Position: 1,2,3

2nd Position: 2,3,4

3rd Position: 3,4,1

4th Position: 4,1,2

ORIGINAL PATTERN

B

FILLS GROOVES

1

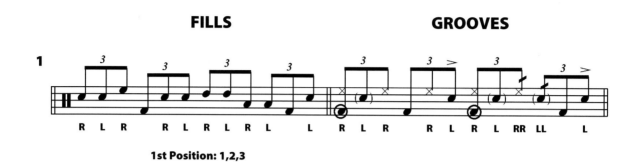

1st Position: 1,2,3

2

2nd Position: 2,3,4

3

3rd Position: 3,4,1

4

4th Position: 4,1,2

ORIGINAL PATTERN

C

30

FILLS   **GROOVES**

1

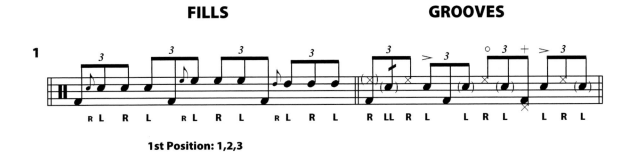

1st Position: 1,2,3

2

31

2nd Position: 2,3,4

3

32

3rd Position: 3,4,1

4

33

4th Position: 4,1,2

ORIGINAL PATTERN

D

R L R   R L L   L R   R L L   L R L

FILLS   GROOVES

1

R L R   R L   L R   R L   R L R   R L   LL R   R L

1st Position: 1,2,3

2

R L   L R   R L   L R L   R L   L R   RR LL   L R L

2nd Position: 2,3,4

3

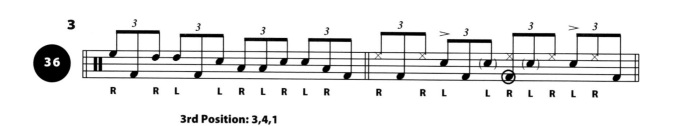

R   R L   L R L R L R   R   R L   L R L R L R

3rd Position: 3,4,1

4

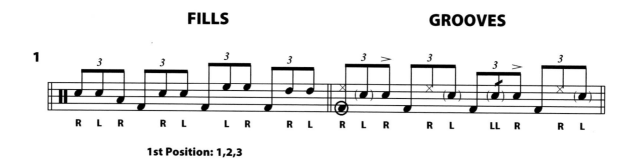

L R L R L R   R L   L   R L R L R L R   R L   LL

4th Position: 4,1,2

ORIGINAL PATTERN

FILLS GROOVES

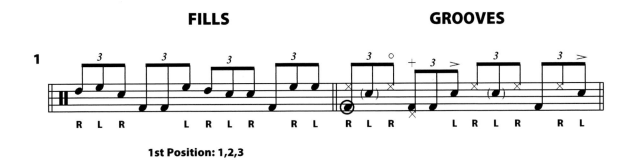

1st Position: 1,2,3

2nd Position: 2,3,4

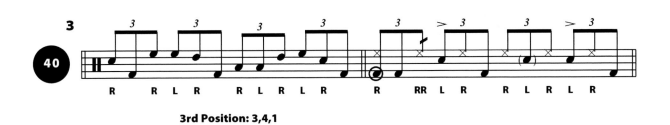

3rd Position: 3,4,1

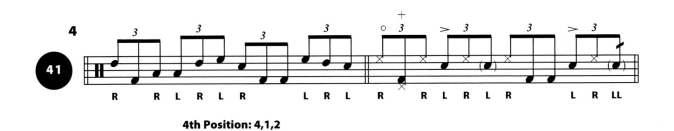

4th Position: 4,1,2

This chapter is divided into two parts, drums fills and grooves.

DRUM FILLS

The following drum fills have two bass drum notes played within four 16th notes (examples A-F). It is important to follow the sticking pattern that is written, as described in the beginning of chapter 2.

GROOVES

Every one of the fills in this chapter can be converted to a groove. Here are the rules to apply:

- Play your right hand on the hi-hat or ride cymbal and left hand on the snare drum.

- Add an optional bass drum or hi-hat on beat 1.

- Accent various snare notes for the backbeat on beats 2 and 4, or other snare notes within the groove for a more displaced-sounding beat.

- Move the right hand from the hi-hat to the snare for an optional backbeat choice.

- Add ghost notes, drags, and open hi-hat patterns to the beats.

- Improvise with various bass drum parts throughout the bar.

PASIC 2009, Indianapolis

ORIGINAL PATTERN

A

42

FILLS   **GROOVES**

1

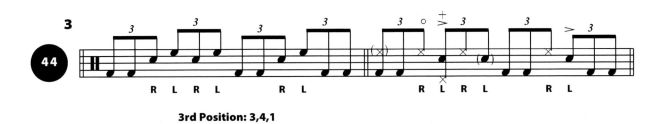

1st Position: 1,2,3

2

43

2nd Position: 2,3,4

3

44

3rd Position: 3,4,1

4

45

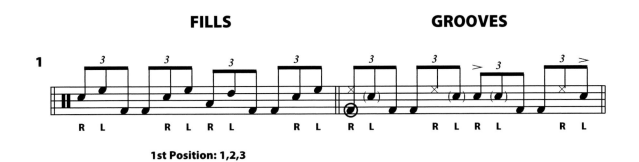

4th Position: 4,1,2

ORIGINAL PATTERN

B

FILLS   GROOVES

1

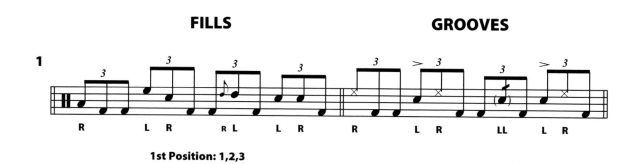

1st Position: 1,2,3

2

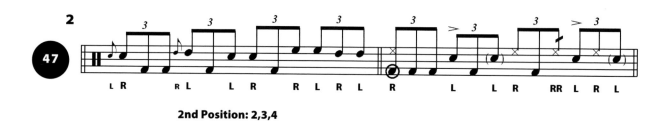

2nd Position: 2,3,4

3

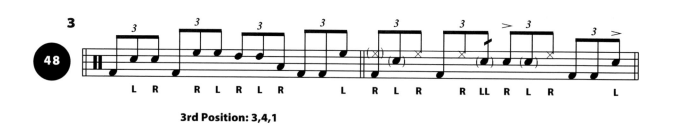

3rd Position: 3,4,1

4

4th Position: 4,1,2

ORIGINAL PATTERN

C

50

L R   L R   L R   R L   R L r L R L

FILLS   GROOVES

1

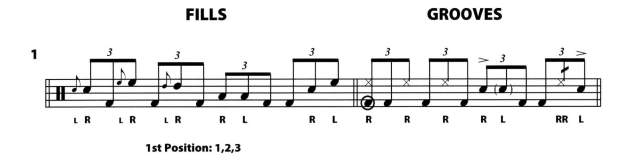

L R   L R   L R   R L   R L   R R R   R L   RR L

1st Position: 1,2,3

2

51

L R   R L   R L R L R L   R   R L   R L R L R L

2nd Position: 2,3,4

3

52

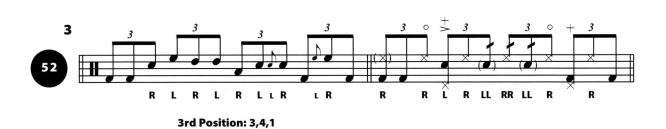

R L R L R LlR   L R   R   R L R LL RR LL R   R

3rd Position: 3,4,1

4

53

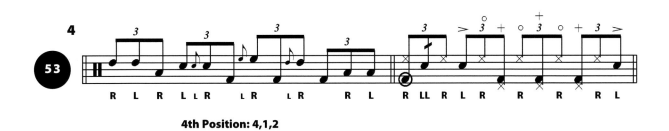

R L R LlR   L R   L R   R L   R LL R L R   R   R   R L

4th Position: 4,1,2

ORIGINAL PATTERN

D

FILLS   GROOVES

1

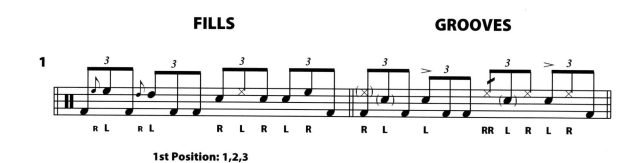

1st Position: 1,2,3

2

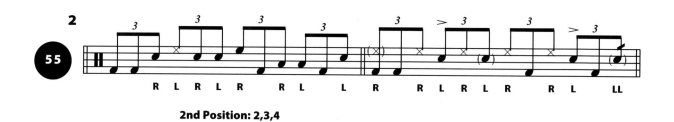

2nd Position: 2,3,4

3

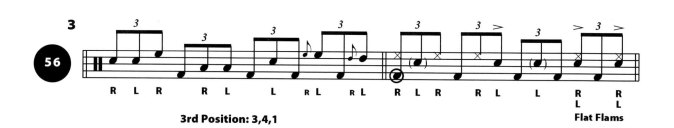

3rd Position: 3,4,1

4

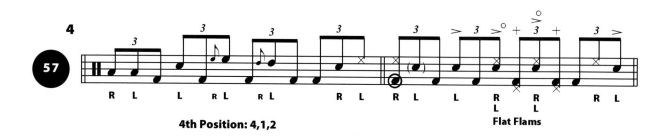

4th Position: 4,1,2

ORIGINAL PATTERN

E

58

R L R L R L R L R L R L

FILLS   **GROOVES**

1

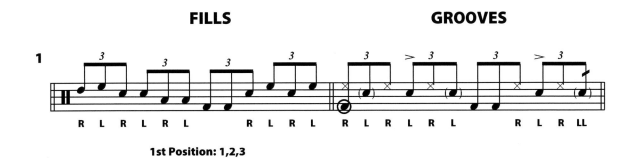

R L R L R L R L R L R L R L R L R L R LL

1st Position: 1,2,3

2

59

R L R L R L R L R L R L R L R L

2nd Position: 2,3,4

3

60

R L R L R L R L R L R L R L R L R L R L

3rd Position: 3,4,1

4

61

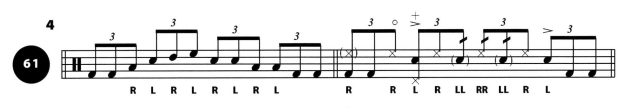

R L R L R L R L R R L R LL RR LL R L

4th Position: 4,1,2

PARADIDDLE IDEAS

In this chapter we will introduce the single paradiddle, paraddidle variations, and double strokes. Letters A1-D1 show groupings of 16th notes with various stickings of the single paradiddle. E1 shows double strokes. When playing these patterns as written, it is very easy to hear and feel the downbeat (every 4th note). The challenge is to play the same patterns as 8th-note triplets. The downbeat will fall every third note, but your new sticking variation begins on every 4th note. This will create a feel of 3 over 4 (the beginning of each patterns starts on the half-note triplet). For exercises A2-E2, I have added the bass drum playing quarter notes to give you the sense of 3 over 4. Practice exercises A2-E2 before moving into the fills and grooves of this chapter. For these exercises, try playing the first note of every four on the toms, and the other notes on the snare (e.g. Aa2).

Also try playing the right hand on the hi-hat or ride cymbal and the left hand on the snare (e.g. Bb2).

PARADIDDLES

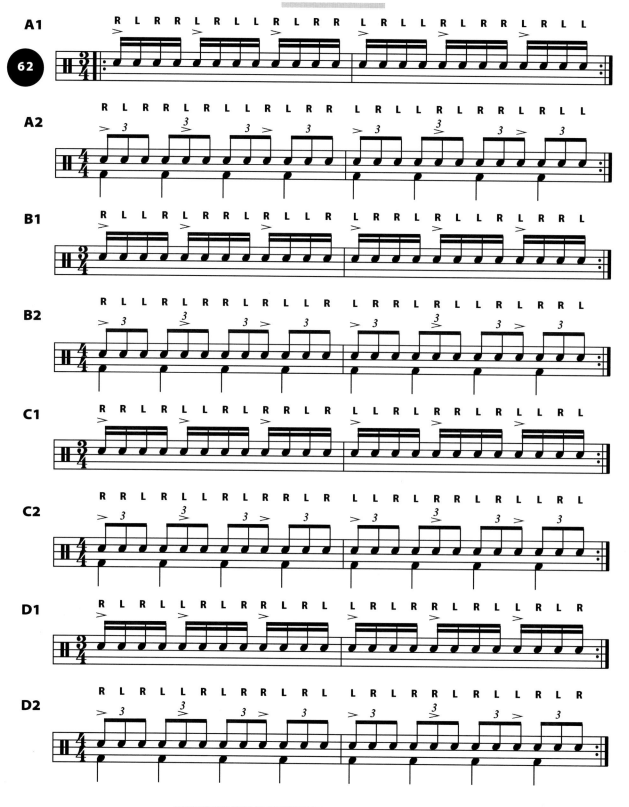

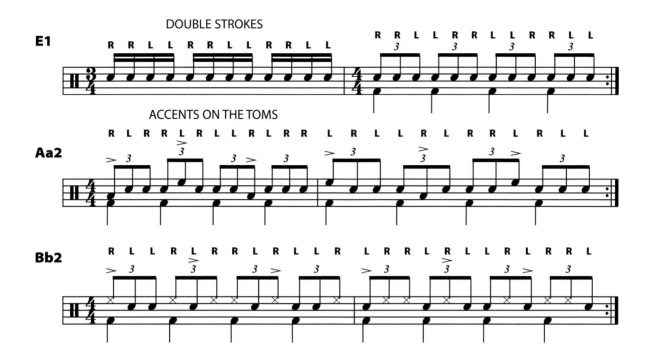

DRUM FILLS

For the fills in this chapter I have left the accents out, as I find that with each variation you will feel different ways to express accents. There are many possibilities. Apply what feels best for you. Try many of the grooves suggested in the back of the book for this chapter, and for a jazzy feel play these with either a 2 or 4 feel with the hi-hat on beats 2 and 4. A great warmup before approaching the one-bar patterns is to try the paradiddle pickup fill ideas which are based on 4 notes (see examples 1a-5d). I have used different groove variations to express these ideas.

PARADIDDLE PICKUP FILL IDEAS

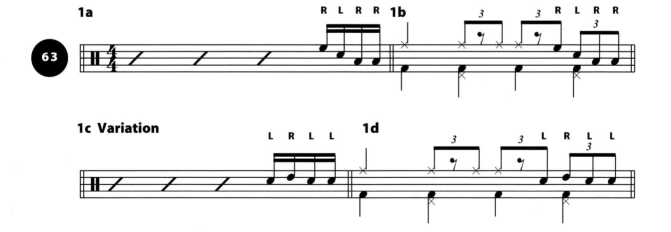

2a

2b

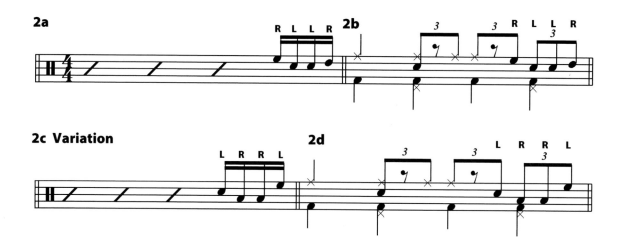

2c Variation

2d

3a

3b

3c

3d

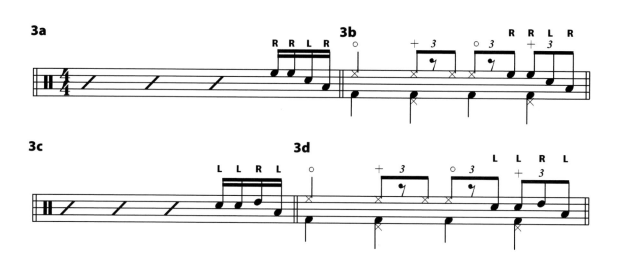

4a

4b

4c

4d

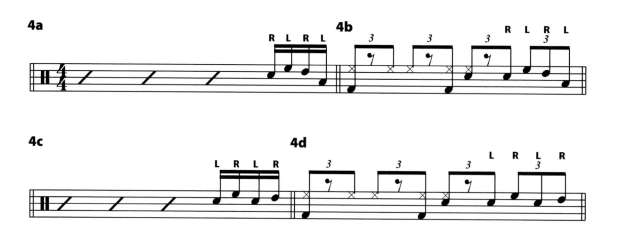

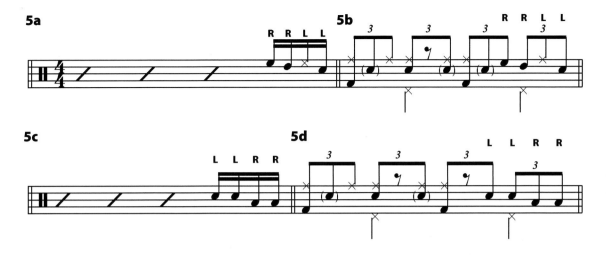

GROOVES AND JAZZ IDEAS

I have converted the following fills into different triplet-based grooves or jazz comping ideas. For many of the jazz ideas, I have written drum figures above the staff to show how the paradiddle idea was transposed to triplets while still playing the original sticking from the 16th-note pattern. I have improvised on the bass drum in these examples. The objective is to get comfortable playing the same sticking pattern voiced and accented around the kit as a fill or a groove both as triplets and 16th notes. These ideas will increase your triplet-based vocabulary.

BASIC STICKING   **DRUM KIT PATTERN**

B

68

R L L R L L R L R R L R L R R L   R L L R L L R L R R L R L R R L

FILLS   **GROOVES AND JAZZ IDEAS**

1

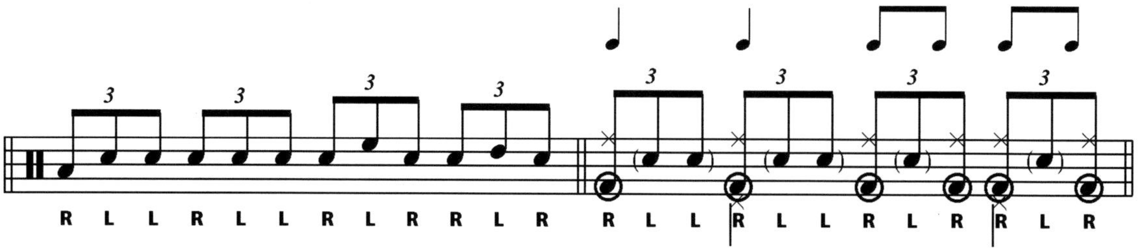

R L L R L L R L R R L R   R L L R L L R L R R L R

1st Position: 1,2,3

2

69

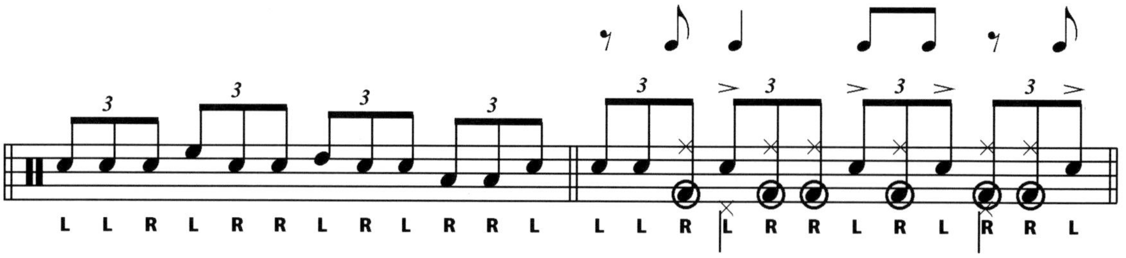

L L R L R R L R L R R L   L L R L R R L R L R R L

2nd Position: 2,3,4

3

70

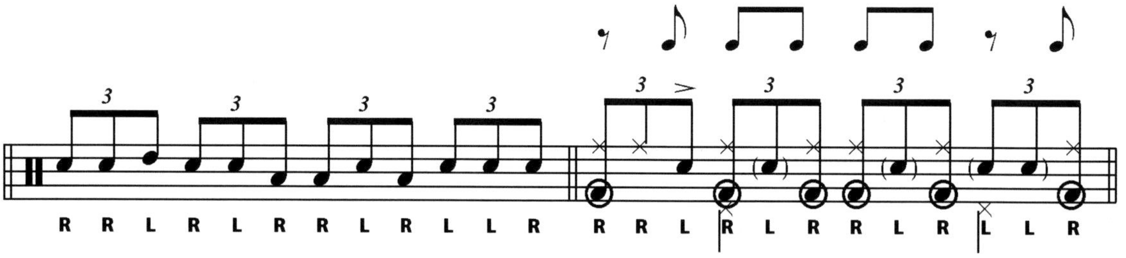

R R L R L R R L R L L R   R R L R L R R L R L L R

3rd Position: 3,4,1

4

71

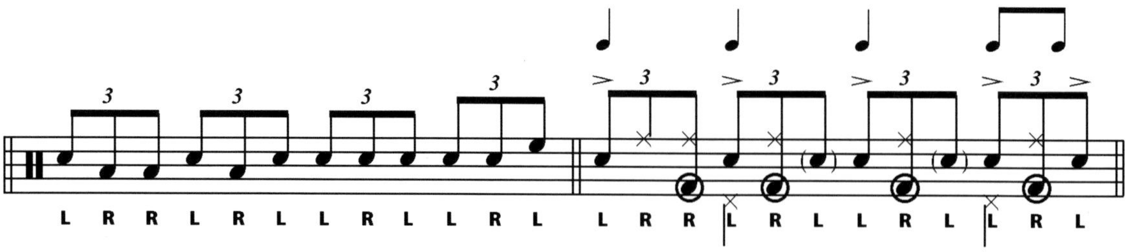

L R R L R L L R L L R L   L R R L R L L R L L R L

4th Position: 4,1,2

BASIC STICKING   **DRUM KIT PATTERN**

R L R R L R L R R L R L R R L R   R L R R L R L R R L R L R R L R

FILLS   **GROOVES AND JAZZ IDEAS**

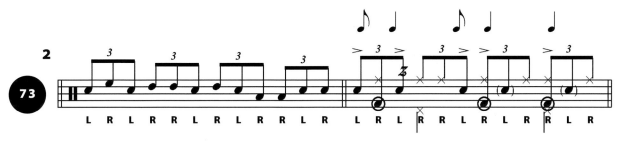

R L R R L R L R R L R L   R L R R L R L R R L R L

1st Position: 1,2,3

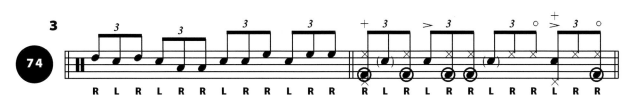

L R L R R L R L R R L R   L R L R R L R L R R L R

2nd Position: 2,3,4

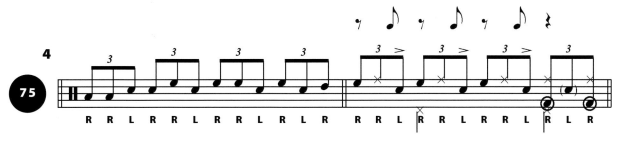

R L R L R R L R L R R R R   R L R L R R L R L R R R

3rd Position: 3,4,1

R R L R R L R R L R L R   R R L R R L R R L R L R

4th Position: 4,1,2

BASIC STICKING **DRUM KIT PATTERN**

D
76

R R L R L R R L R L L L R L R L L   R R L R L R R L R L L L R L R L L

FILLS **GROOVES AND JAZZ IDEAS**

1
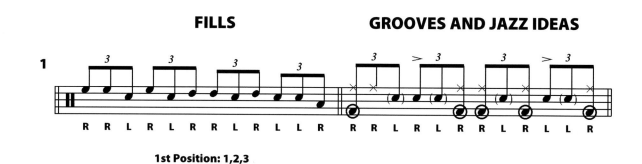

R R L R L R R L R L L R   R R L R L R R L R L L R

1st Position: 1,2,3

2
77

L R R L R L L L R L R L L   L R R L R L L L R L R L L

2nd Position: 2,3,4

3
78
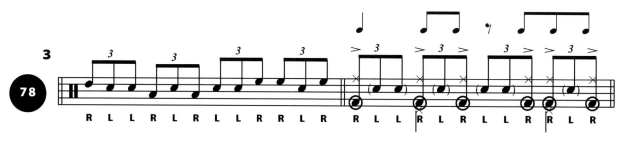

R L L L R L R L L R R L R   R L L L R L R L L R R L R

3rd Position: 3,4,1

4
79

L R L L R R L R L R R L   L R L L R R L R L R R L

4th Position: 4,1,2

BASIC STICKING   **DRUM KIT PATTERN**

E

80

L R L R L L R R L R L L R R L   L R L L R L L R R L R L L R R L

FILLS   **GROOVES AND JAZZ IDEAS**

1

L R L L L R L L R R L R L   L R L L R L L R R R L R L

1st Position: 1,2,3

2

81

R L L R R L R L L R R L   R L L R R L R L L R R L

2nd Position: 2,3,4

3

82

R L R L L R R L L R L L   R L R L L R R L L R L L

3rd Position: 3,4,1

4

83

L R R L L R L L R L L R   L R R L L R L L R L L R

4th Position: 4,1,2

CHAPTER 5

COMBINATION FILL AND GROOVE IDEAS

This chapter contains a combination of ideas and patterns used in chapters 1-4. You will notice quite a wide range and variety of fills and grooves with many of the different sticking patterns combined together. Many of the grooves have influences of reggae and Afro-Cuban flavors, as well as shuffle and jazz ideas from the previous chapters.

BASIC STICKING   **DRUM KIT PATTERN**

FILLS   **GROOVES AND JAZZ IDEAS**

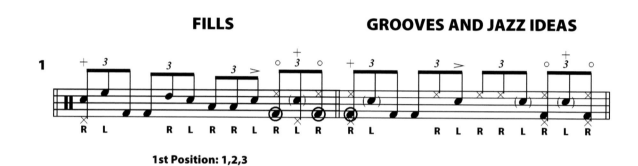

1st Position: 1,2,3

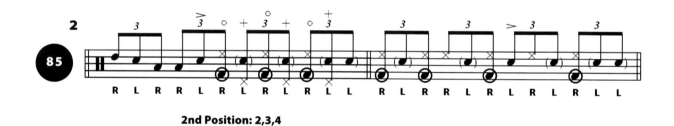

2nd Position: 2,3,4

3rd Position: 3,4,1

4th Position: 4,1,2

BASIC STICKING

DRUM KIT PATTERN

B

88

R R L R L R L L   L R   R   R L   R R L R L R L L   L R   L R   R L

FILLS

GROOVES AND JAZZ IDEAS

1

R R L R L R L L   L R   R R L R L R L L   L R

1st Position: 1,2,3

SPLASH CYMBAL

2

89

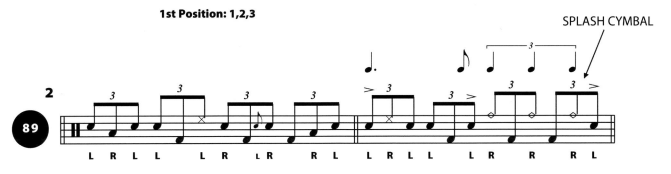

L R L L   L R   L R   R L   L R L L   L R   R   R L

2nd Position: 2,3,4

3

90

L R   L R   R L R R L R   R L R   R   R L R R L R

3rd Position: 3,4,1

4

91

L R   R L R R L R L R L L   R   R L R R L R L R L L

4th Position: 4,1,2

BASIC STICKING

DRUM KIT PATTERN

C

92

FILLS

GROOVES AND JAZZ IDEAS

1

1st Position: 1,2,3

2

93

2nd Position: 2,3,4

3

94

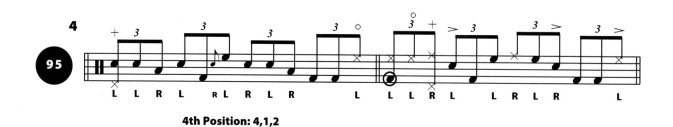

3rd Position: 3,4,1

4

95

4th Position: 4,1,2

BASIC STICKING   **DRUM KIT PATTERN**

D

96

R L L R L R R L L R L R   R L R L L R L R R L L R L R   R L

FILLS   **GROOVES AND JAZZ IDEAS**

1

R L L R L R R L L R L R   R L L R L R R L L R L R

1st Position: 1,2,3

2

97

L R R L L R L R   R L   L R R L L R L R   R L

2nd Position: 2,3,4

3

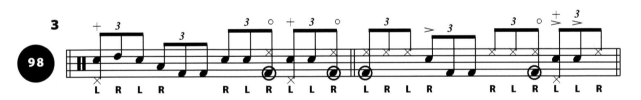

98

L R L R   R L R L L R   L R L R   R L R L L R

3rd Position: 3,4,1

4

99

R L R L L R L R R L   R   R L R L L R L R R

4th Position: 4,1,2

BASIC STICKING   **DRUM KIT PATTERN**

E

100

R R R L L L R L R L R L   L R R L R L L R R L R L R L

FILLS   **GROOVES AND JAZZ IDEAS**

1

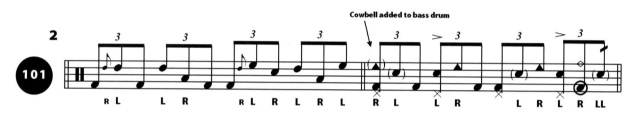

L R R L R L L R R L R R L L L R L

1st Position: 1,2,3

2

101

Cowbell added to bass drum

R L L R R L R L R L R L L R L R L R LL

2nd Position: 2,3,4

3

102

R R L R L R L L R   R L R L R LL R L R R L

3rd Position: 3,4,1

4

103

R L R L L R R L R L L R L R L R R LL L L

4th Position: 4,1,2

Sixteenth-Note Rhythms Converted To Eighth-Note Triplets

In this chapter, things get more interesting as we take 15 various 16th-note rhythms from 1 to 4 notes and rewrite them as 8th-note triplets.

Let's take a look at rhythm B1:

The above rhythm consists of two 16th notes followed by an 8th note. Basically, if we count in 16th notes then we would play the first three notes and rest on the fourth. If we switch to 3/4 time and triplets, but play the same sequence (play three notes & rest on the fourth), we get a totally different result.

Written below are 15 different rhythms transposed to 8th-note triplets. Start off slow and count out loud. Pay attention to the sticking patterns.

FILLS WITH RESTS

BASIC PATTERN
DRUM KIT PATTERN

A
107

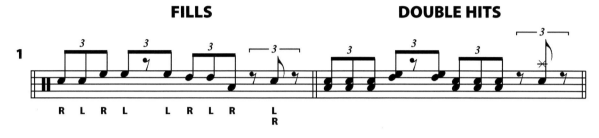

R L R L   L R L R   R   R L R
                  R   L

R L R L   L R L R   R   R L R
                  R   L

FILLS
DOUBLE HITS

1

R L R L   L R L R   L
                       R

1st Position: 1,2,3

2
108

L R L R   R   R L R
              L

2nd Position: 2,3,4

3
109

R   R   R L R   R L R L
     L

3rd Position: 3,4,1

4
110

R L R   R L R L   L R L

4th Position: 4,1,2

BASIC STICKING

DRUM KIT PATTERN

B

111

R L   L R   R L   L R L R L R   R R L   L R   R L   L R L R L R

FILLS

DOUBLE HITS

1

R R L   L R   R L   L R L

1st Position: 1,2,3

2

112

R   R L   L R L R L R

2nd Position: 2,3,4

3

113

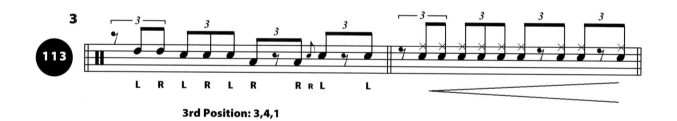

L R   L R   L R   R R L   L

3rd Position: 3,4,1

4

114

R L R   R R L   L R   R L

4th Position: 4,1,2

BASIC STICKING　　　　　**DRUM KIT PATTERN**

FILLS　　　　　**DOUBLE HITS**

1st Position: 1,2,3

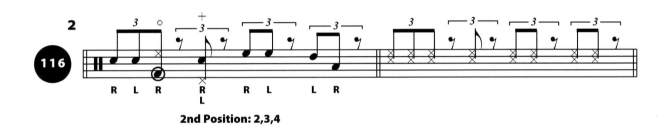

2nd Position: 2,3,4

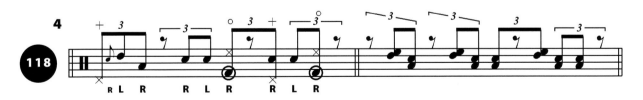

3rd Position: 3,4,1

4th Position: 4,1,2

BASIC STICKING　　　　　　　**DRUM KIT PATTERN**

FILLS　　　　　　　　**DOUBLE HITS**

1st Position: 1,2,3

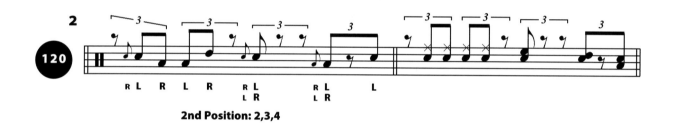

2nd Position: 2,3,4

3rd Position: 3,4,1

4th Position: 4,1,2

BASIC STICKING   DRUM KIT PATTERN

E

123

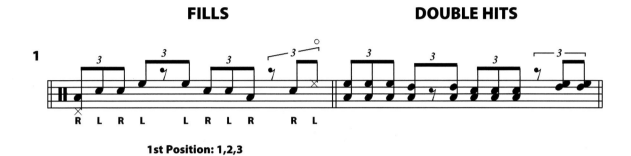

R L R L   L R L R   R L   R L

FILLS   DOUBLE HITS

1

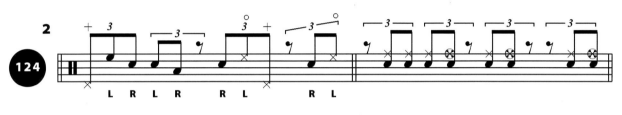

R L R L   L R L R   R L

1st Position: 1,2,3

2

124

L R L R   R L   R L

2nd Position: 2,3,4

3

125

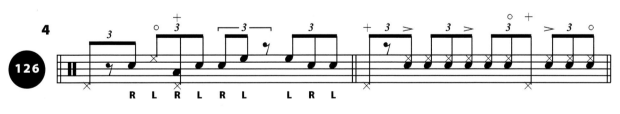

R   R L   R L R L R L

3rd Position: 3,4,1

4

126

R L R L R L   L R L

4th Position: 4,1,2

FOOT OSTINATOS

Once you are comfortable with the previous examples, try these foot ostinatos 1-6. Theses fills are great to apply to the many grooves listed in this book.

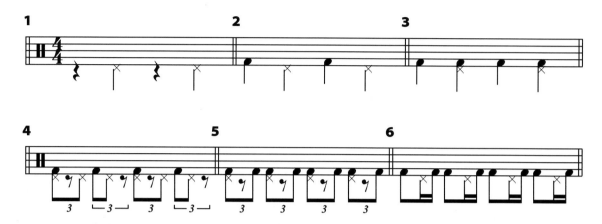

Drums Live 2005. "What's so funny?"

In this chapter we will introduce 32nd notes and show how they are converted to 16th-note-triplet rhythms.

WARM-UP EXERCISES

Each of these examples demonstrates one bar of 16th notes in 3/4 time and how it would be played in 4/4 time as triplets. Try playing both written examples at the same speed but changing the way you count the rhythms. Start at 60 BPM, keeping the pulse falling on the first of every four notes. When you are playing the triplets, the metronome will fall on the half-note triplet. Count out loud, and try adding quarter notes on the bass drum. This will give you the feel of 3 over 4. See example A1 and A2.

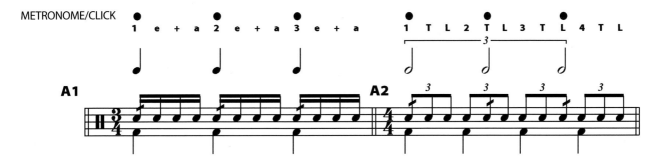

Examples A-O are 15 various 16th-note patterns that I have added 32nd notes to. It is important to follow the sticking pattern written (if you are left handed play the opposite sticking). We will use these rhythms to create fills with both 8th-note triplets and 16th-note triplets. Before you proceed with the fill combinations, practice warming up with examples A1/A2–O1/O2.

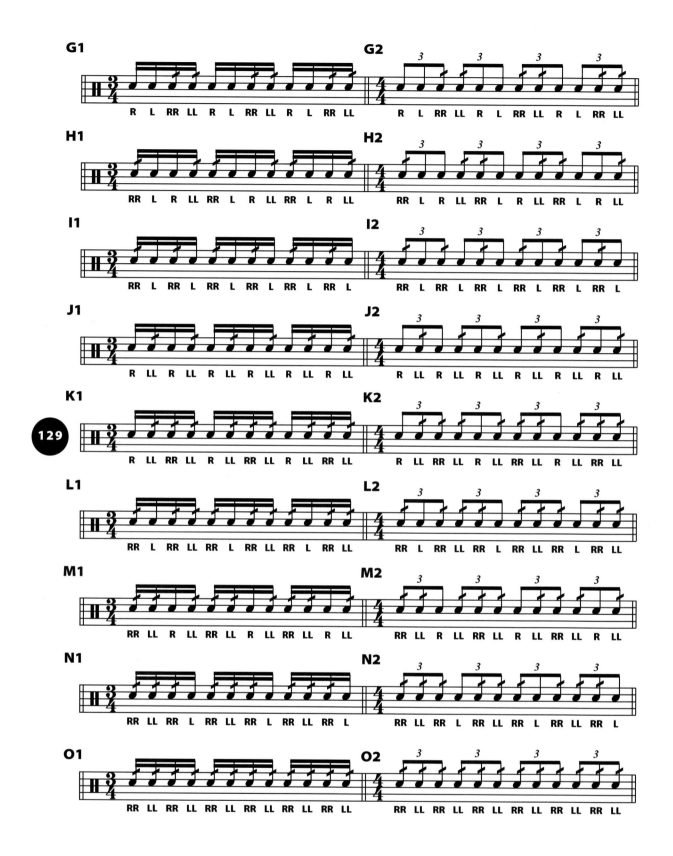

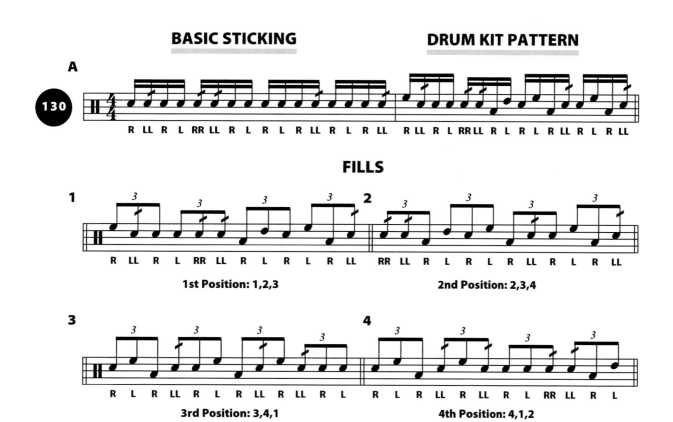

BASIC STICKING   **DRUM KIT PATTERN**

A

130

R LL R L RR LL R L R L R LL R L R LL   R LL R L RR LL R L R L R LL R L R LL

FILLS

1   **2**

R LL R L RR LL R L R L R L R LL   RR LL R L R L R L R LL R L R L R LL

1st Position: 1,2,3   **2nd Position: 2,3,4**

3   **4**

R L R LL R L R LL R LL R L   R L R LL R LL R L RR LL R L

3rd Position: 3,4,1   **4th Position: 4,1,2**

Montreal Drumfest 2009: Roland's electronic drum village

BASIC STICKING   **DRUM KIT PATTERN**

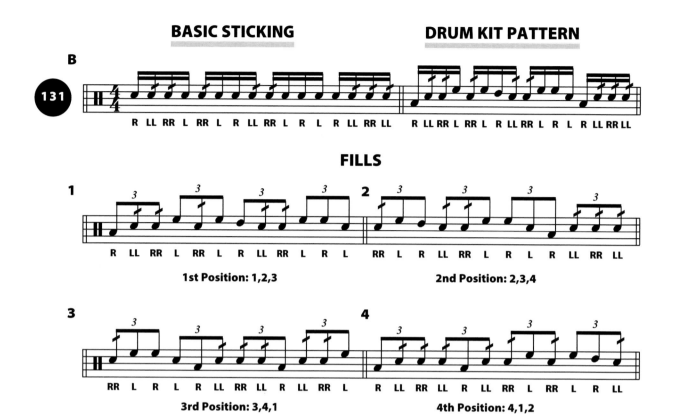

FILLS

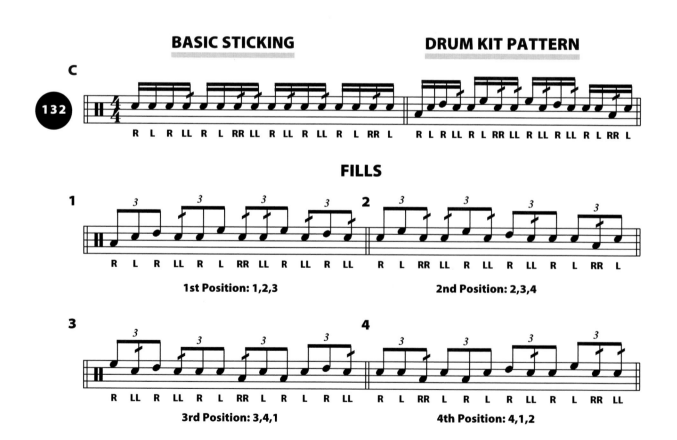

BASIC STICKING

DRUM KIT PATTERN

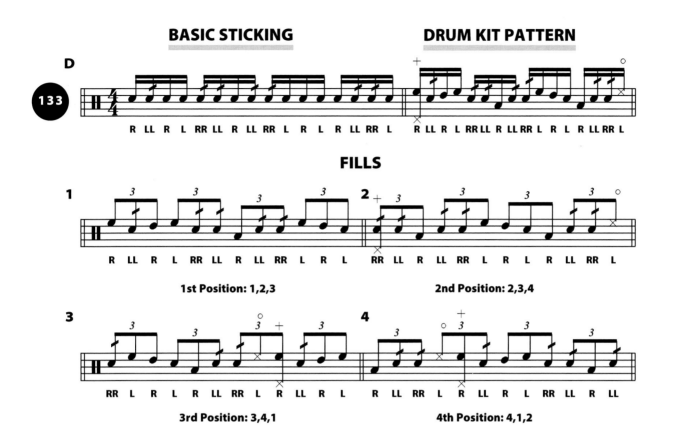

D

133

R LL R L RR LL R LL RR L R L R LL RR L

R LL R L RR LL R LL RR L R L R LL RR L

FILLS

1
R L LL R L RR LL R LL RR L R L

2
RR LL R LL RR L R L R LL RR L

1st Position: 1,2,3

2nd Position: 2,3,4

3
RR L R L R LL RR L R LL R L

4
R LL RR L R LL R L RR LL R LL

3rd Position: 3,4,1

4th Position: 4,1,2

BASIC STICKING

DRUM KIT PATTERN

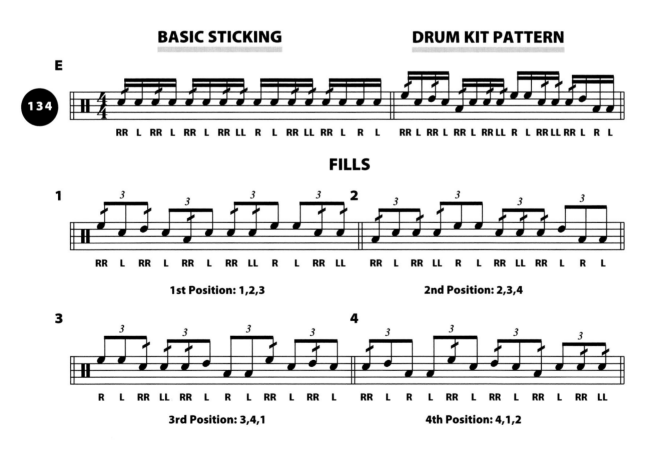

E

134

RR L RR L RR L RR LL R L RR LL RR L R L

RR L RR L RR L RR LL R L RR LL RR L R L

FILLS

1
RR L RR L RR L RR LL R L RR LL

2
RR L RR LL R L RR LL RR L R L

1st Position: 1,2,3

2nd Position: 2,3,4

3
R L RR LL RR L R L RR L RR L

4
RR L R L RR L RR L RR L RR LL

3rd Position: 3,4,1

4th Position: 4,1,2

COMBINATION IDEAS, FILLS AND GROOVES

In this chapter we will combine rhythms from the previous chapters to create fills and groove ideas. As we combine a variety of rhythms, you will see and hear the unique results that come from one basic pattern.

You will notice I have added flams, drags, bass drums, ride cymbal parts and hi-hat notes to certain fills and grooves. Experiment with your own. These ideas are like adding the candles on the cake!

BASIC STICKING   **DRUM KIT PATTERN**

FILLS   **GROOVES AND JAZZ IDEAS**

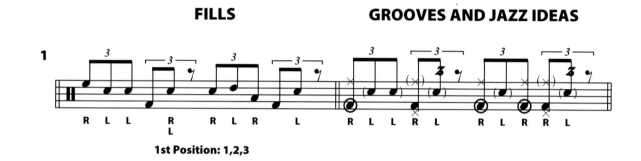

1st Position: 1,2,3

2nd Position: 2,3,4

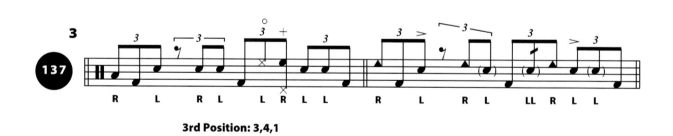

3rd Position: 3,4,1

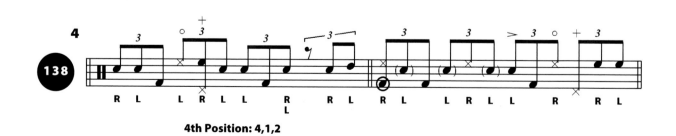

4th Position: 4,1,2

BASIC STICKING   **DRUM KIT PATTERN**

B

139

R R L R L L R L R R R L   R R L R L L R L R R R L

FILLS   **GROOVES AND JAZZ IDEAS**

1

R R L R L L R L R   R R L R L L R L R

1st Position: 1,2,3

2

140

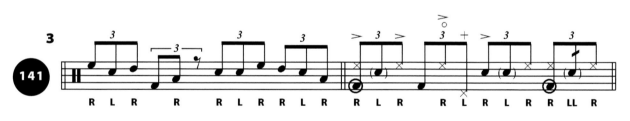

L L R L R R R L   R L L R L R R R L

2nd Position: 2,3,4

3

141

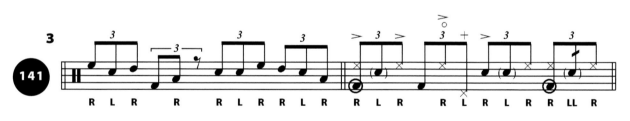

R L R R R L R R L R   R L R R L R L R R LL R

3rd Position: 3,4,1

4

142

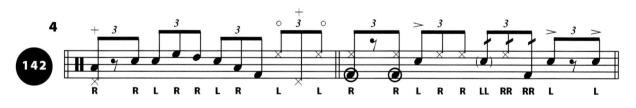

R R L R R L R L L   R R L R R L LL RR RR L L

4th Position: 4,1,2

BASIC STICKING   **DRUM KIT PATTERN**

C

143

R LL RR L R   R   L R L R L L R   R LL RR L R   R   L R L R L L R
         L   L

FILLS   **GROOVES AND JAZZ IDEAS**

1

R LL RR L R   R   L R L   R LL RR L R   R   L R L

1st Position: 1,2,3

2

144

L   R   L R L R L L R   R   R   R L R L R L L R

2nd Position: 2,3,4

3

145

L R L R L L R R LL RR L   R L R L R L L R R LL RR L

3rd Position: 3,4,1

4

146

R L L L R R LL RR L R   L R   R L L L R R LL R L R   R

4th Position: 4,1,2

BASIC STICKING

DRUM KIT PATTERN

D

147

L R L L RL R L RL R L   L   L R L   L R L L RL L R RL R L   L   L R L

FILLS

GROOVES AND JAZZ IDEAS

1

L R L L RL R L RL R L   L   L R L L RL R L RL R L   L

1st Position: 1,2,3

2

148

RL R L RL R L   L   L R L   RL R L RL R L   R L   L R L

2nd Position: 2,3,4

3

149

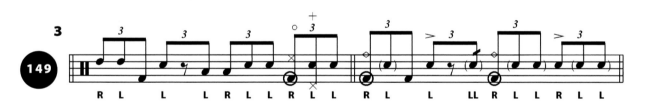

R L   L   L R L L R L L   R L   L   LL R L L R L L

3rd Position: 3,4,1

4

150

L R L L R L L R RL R L RL   L R L L R L L RL R L RL

4th Position: 4,1,2

BASIC STICKING **DRUM KIT PATTERN**

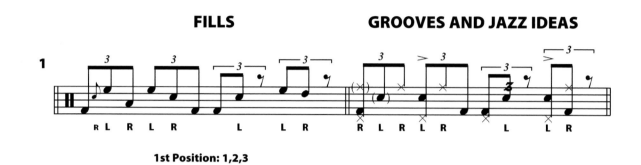

FILLS **GROOVES AND JAZZ IDEAS**

1st Position: 1,2,3

2nd Position: 2,3,4

3rd Position: 3,4,1

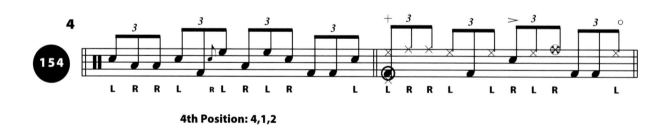

4th Position: 4,1,2

In this section I have written different types of triplet-based grooves on several styles, including blues, shuffles, jazz, reggae, Afro-Cuban, and more. For the shuffle and blues 12/8 grooves, I have written them on ride cymbal. Please try these grooves on the hi-hat as well. These are just a few examples; there are many many more variations. These grooves and fills will give you a good foundation in many popular triplet-based styles.

When applying these grooves with the fills throughout the book, play any one groove for three bars, and for the fourth bar, apply any one of the drum fills. The fills in this book will work with all the grooves and styles I have written. The fills that have been transposed from the original pattern will also work with the transposed grooves. Experiment with different tempos. I have listed a tempo range that these grooves are most commonly heard and played at.

Have fun and enjoy these rhythmic twists!

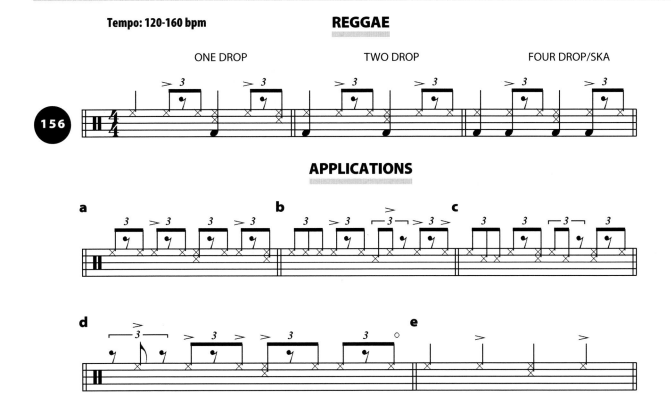

Tempo: 100-240 bpm

JAZZ

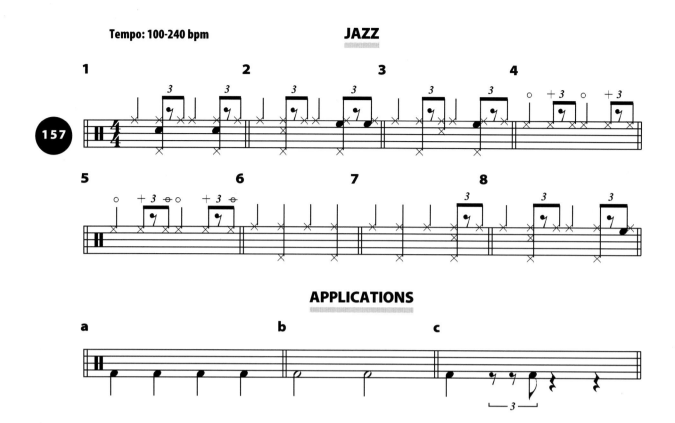

APPLICATIONS

Tempo: 120-160 bpm

AFRO-CUBAN

Tempo: 120-220 bpm

DOUBLE BASS

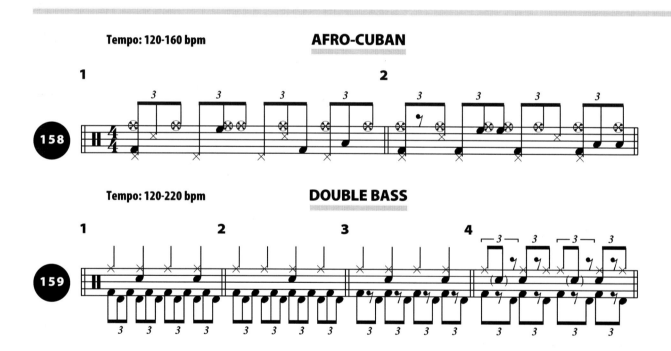

Tempo: 50-120 bpm

BLUES - 12/8 FEEL

160

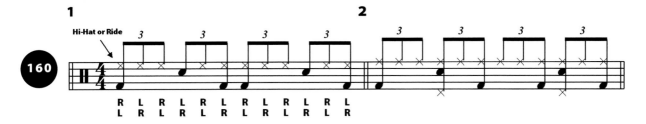

R L R L R L R L R L R L
L R L R L R L R L R L R

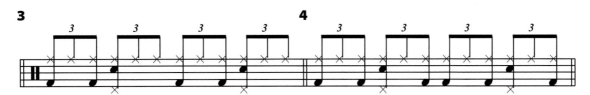

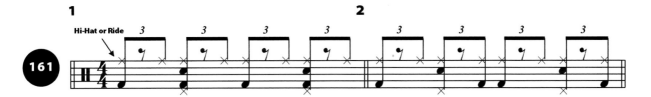

Tempo: 100-160 bpm

SHUFFLES

161

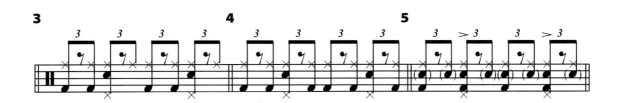

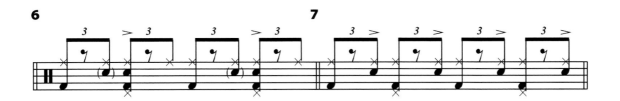

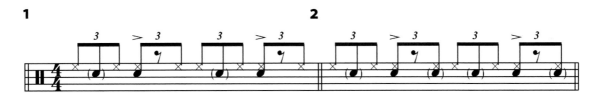

Tempo: 100-160 bpm

GHOST NOTE APPLICATIONS

Tempo: 180-220 bpm

NEW ORLEANS

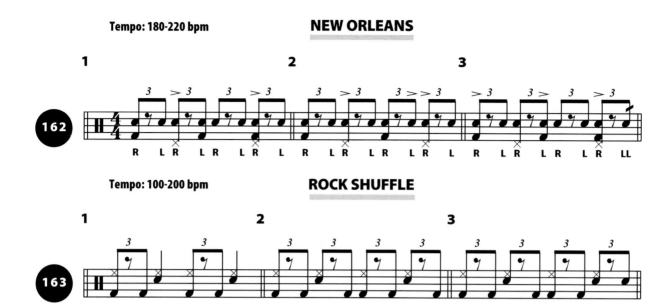

Tempo: 100-200 bpm

ROCK SHUFFLE

Tempo: 140-180 bpm

HALF-TIME SHUFFLE

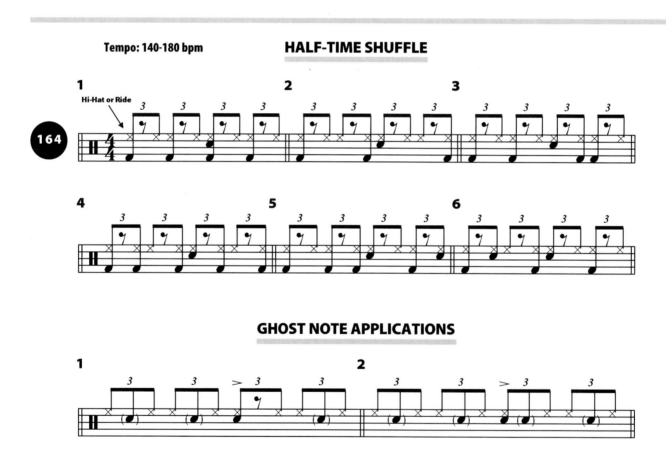

GHOST NOTE APPLICATIONS

RECOMMENDED BOOKS AND DVDs
Featuring Triplet-Based Grooves, Fills and Play-Along Songs

Groove Essentials 1.0 & 2.0 book and DVD by Tommy Igoe (Hudson Music)

The Art of Bop Drumming and *Beyond Bop Drumming* book by John Riley (Alfred Publishing Co.)

Baby Steps to Giant Steps book by Peter Retzlaff and Jim Rupp (Hudson Music)

The Drummers Guide to Shuffles book by Dee Potter (Hal Leonard)

Polyrhythmic Creativity on the Drumset book by Paul Delong (Hudson Music)

The New Method of Afro-Cuban Drumming book by Jimmy Branly (Hudson Music)

Reggae for the Drumset digital download by Lerryns Hernandez (Hudson Limited)

Drum Legacy: Standing on the Shoulders of Giants DVD by Steve Smith (Hudson Music)

The Art of Playing with Brushes DVD (Hudson Music)

Beyond the Chops DVD by Aaron Spears (Hudson Music)

Drumset Technique and History of the U.S. Beat DVD by Steve Smith (Hudson Music)

Musical Drumming in Different Styles DVD by Gregg Bissonette (Hudson Music)

Drummers Guide to Hip-Hop book by Bill Elder (Alfred Publishing Co.)

Linear Time Playing book by Gary Chaffee (Alfred Publishing Co.)

The Commandments of R&B Drumming book by Zoro (Alfred Publishing Co.)

Early Rhythm & Blues Drumming book by Zoro and Daniel Glass (Alfred Publishing Co.)

Rick's Licks book by Rick Gratton (Alfred Publishing Co.)

Afro-Cuban Coordination for Drumset book by Maria Martinez (Hal Leonard)

DVD/BOOKS ON TECHNIQUE

Secret Weapons for the Modern Drummer DVD by JoJo Mayer (Hudson Music)

Great Hands for a Lifetime DVD by Tommy Igoe (Hudson Music)

It's Your Move book by Dom Famularo with Joe Bergamini (Alfred Publishing Co.)

The Weaker Side book by Dom Famularo and Stephane Chamberland (Alfred Publishing Co.)

Modern Reading Text in 4/4 Time book by Louie Bellson (Alfred Publishing Co.)

Master Studies book by Joe Morello (Modern Drummer Publications)

Syncopation book by Ted Reed (Alfred Publishing Co.)

Stick Control book by George Lawrence Stone (Alfred Publishing Co.)

CONCLUSION

Congratulations! You have reached the end, and by this point you will probably will forget how to play a straight 8th-note groove and drum fill! (Just kidding.)

You have now expanded your triplet vocabulary with several new ideas and concepts that I hope you can utilize in your everyday practicing and performance.

My goal was to get you comfortable and thinking outside the box with new, creative fills, grooves, and timing ideas that can be applied in any triplet-based style of music.

Please visit me at www.salemdrum.com and share with me some of your own rhythmic twists.

Have fun!